Table of Contents

Success Strategies

This section contains a list of test-taking strategies that you may find helpful as you work through the test. By taking what you know and applying logical thought, you can maximize your chances of answering any question correctly!

It is very important to realize that every question is different and every person is different: no single strategy will work on every question, and no single strategy will work for every person. That's why we've included all of them here, so you can try them out and determine which ones work best for different types of questions and which ones work best for you.

Question Strategies

Read Carefully

Read the question and answer choices carefully. Don't miss the question because you misread the terms. You have plenty of time to read each question thoroughly and make sure you understand what is being asked. Yet a happy medium must be attained, so don't waste too much time. You must read carefully, but efficiently.

Contextual Clues

Look for contextual clues. If the question includes a word you are not familiar with, look at the immediate context for some indication of what the word might mean. Contextual clues can often give you all the information you need to decipher the meaning of an unfamiliar word. Even if you can't determine the meaning, you may be able to narrow down the possibilities enough to make a solid guess at the answer to the question.

Prefixes

If you're having trouble with a word in the question or answer choices, try dissecting it. Take advantage of every clue that the word might include. Prefixes and suffixes can be a huge help. Usually they allow you to determine a basic meaning. Pre- means before, post- means after, pro - is positive, de- is negative. From prefixes and suffixes, you can get an idea of the general meaning of the word and try to put it into context.

Hedge Words

Watch out for critical hedge words, such as *likely, may, can, often, almost, mostly, usually, generally, rarely,* and *sometimes.* Question writers insert these hedge phrases to cover every possibility. Often an answer choice will be wrong simply because it leaves no room for exception. Be on guard for answer choices that have definitive words such as *exactly* and *always.*

Switchback Words

Stay alert for *switchbacks.* These are the words and phrases frequently used to alert you to shifts in thought. The most common switchback words are *but, although,* and *however.* Others include *nevertheless, on the other hand, even though, while, in spite of, despite, regardless of.* Switchback words are important to catch because they can change the direction of the question or an answer choice.

Face Value

When in doubt, use common sense. Accept the situation in the problem at face value. Don't read too much into it. These problems will not require you to make wild assumptions. If you have to go beyond creativity and warp time or space in order to have an answer choice fit the question, then you should move on and consider the other answer choices. These are normal problems rooted in reality. The applicable relationship or explanation may not be readily apparent, but it is there for you to figure out. Use your common sense to interpret anything that isn't clear.

Answer Choice Strategies

Answer Selection

The most thorough way to pick an answer choice is to identify and eliminate wrong answers until only one is left, then confirm it is the correct answer. Sometimes an answer choice may immediately seem right, but be careful. The test writers will usually put more than one reasonable answer choice on each question, so take a second to read all of them and make sure that the other choices are not equally obvious. As long as you have time left, it is better to read every answer choice than to pick the first one that looks right without checking the others.

Answer Choice Families

An answer choice family consists of two (in rare cases, three) answer choices that are very similar in construction and cannot all be true at the same time. If you see two answer choices that are direct opposites or parallels, one of them is usually the correct answer. For instance, if one answer choice says that quantity *x* increases and another either says that quantity *x* decreases (opposite) or says that quantity *y* increases (parallel), then those answer choices would fall into the same family. An answer choice that doesn't match the construction of the answer choice family is more likely to be incorrect. Most questions will not have answer choice families, but when they do appear, you should be prepared to recognize them.

Eliminate Answers

Eliminate answer choices as soon as you realize they are wrong, but make sure you consider all possibilities. If you are eliminating answer choices and realize that the last one you are left with is also wrong, don't panic. Start over and consider each choice again. There may be something you missed the first time that you will realize on the second pass.

Avoid Fact Traps

Don't be distracted by an answer choice that is factually true but doesn't answer the question. You are looking for the choice that answers the question. Stay focused on what the question is asking for so you don't accidentally pick an answer that is true but incorrect. Always go back to the question and make sure the answer choice you've selected actually answers the question and is not merely a true statement.

Extreme Statements

In general, you should avoid answers that put forth extreme actions as standard practice or proclaim controversial ideas as established fact. An answer choice that states the "process should be used in certain situations, if..." is much more likely to be correct than one that states the "process should be discontinued completely." The first is a calm rational statement and doesn't even make a definitive, uncompromising stance, using a hedge word *if* to provide wiggle room, whereas the second choice is a radical idea and far more extreme.

Benchmark

As you read through the answer choices and you come across one that seems to answer the question well, mentally select that answer choice. This is not your final answer, but it's the one that will help you evaluate the other answer choices. The one that you selected is your benchmark or standard for judging each of the other answer choices. Every other answer choice must be compared to your benchmark. That choice is correct until proven otherwise by another answer choice beating it. If you find a better answer, then that one becomes your new benchmark. Once you've decided that no other choice answers the question as well as your benchmark, you have your final answer.

Predict the Answer

Before you even start looking at the answer choices, it is often best to try to predict the answer. When you come up with the answer on your own, it is easier to avoid distractions and traps because you will know exactly what to look for. The right answer choice is unlikely to be word-for-word what you came up with, but it should be a close match. Even if you are confident that you have the right answer, you should still take the time to read each option before moving on.

General Strategies

Tough Questions

If you are stumped on a problem or it appears too hard or too difficult, don't waste time. Move on! Remember though, if you can quickly check for obviously incorrect answer choices, your chances of guessing correctly are greatly improved. Before you completely give up, at least try to knock out a couple of possible answers. Eliminate what you can and then guess at the remaining answer choices before moving on.

Check Your Work

Since you will probably not know every term listed and the answer to every question, it is important that you get credit for the ones that you do know.

Don't miss any questions through careless mistakes. If at all possible, try to take a second to look back over your answer selection and make sure you've selected the correct answer choice and haven't made a costly careless mistake (such as marking an answer choice that you didn't mean to mark). This quick double check should more than pay for itself in caught mistakes for the time it costs.

Pace Yourself

It's easy to be overwhelmed when you're looking at a page full of questions; your mind is confused and full of random thoughts, and the clock is ticking down faster than you would like. Calm down and maintain the pace that you have set for yourself. Especially as you get down to the last few minutes of the test, don't let the small numbers on the clock make you panic. As long as you are on track by monitoring your pace, you are guaranteed to have time for each question.

Don't Rush

It is very easy to make errors when you are in a hurry. Maintaining a fast pace in answering questions is pointless if it makes you miss questions that you would have gotten right otherwise. Test writers like to include distracting information and wrong answers that seem right. Taking a little extra time to avoid careless mistakes can make all the difference in your test score. Find a pace that allows you to be confident in the answers that you select.

Keep Moving

Panicking will not help you pass the test, so do your best to stay calm and keep moving. Taking deep breaths and going through the answer elimination steps you practiced can help to break through a stress barrier and keep your pace.

Final Notes

The combination of a solid foundation of content knowledge and the confidence that comes from practicing your plan for applying that knowledge is the key to maximizing your performance on test day. As your foundation of content knowledge is built up and strengthened, you'll find that the strategies included in this chapter become more and more effective in helping you quickly sift through the distractions and traps of the test to isolate the correct answer.

Now it's time to move on to the test content chapters of this book, but be sure to keep your goal in mind. As you read, think about how you will be able to apply this information on the test. If you've already seen sample questions for the test and you have an idea of the question format and style, try to come up with questions of your own that you can answer based on what you're reading. This will give you valuable practice applying your knowledge in the same ways you can expect to on test day.

Good luck and good studying!

Reading: Literature

Key Ideas and Details

Chapter 1: Mom's Big Idea

1 "This has got to stop!"

2 Janey could tell that her mom was exasperated. She watched from the hallway as her mother stared out the living room window as one car after another whizzed by their house.

3 "What's wrong, Mom?" Janey asked.

4 "These cars and trucks flying down the road, that's what. It's dangerous, and if something isn't done about it someone is going to get run over one of these days. It's just a matter of time. The city needs to lower the speed limit to 35 miles per hour. A few years ago, when there were very few houses out here, a speed limit of 55 miles per hour was fine, but not anymore. We've got to do something about this."

5 "Why don't you call City Hall and ask them to change the speed limit?"

6 "I already have, Janey. I've called several times, I've emailed, and I've even gone down there in person, but I can't get anyone to do anything about the problem. It's like nobody down there cares."

7 Janey was curious. "What are you going to do, Mom?"

8 "I'm not sure yet. I'll have to ponder it for a while."

9 Just then Janey's father pulled into the driveway. "Janey, Dad's home. Finish setting the table."

10 "Okay, Mom."

11 In a few minutes the family was gathered around the table for dinner. Janey listened as her mother and father discussed the problem of the speeding cars at length. As they were clearing the table, Janey asked her mom if she had come up with any ideas yet. Her mom said she had a great idea.

12 "What is it, Mom? Are you going to write a letter to the newspaper? Are you going to protest in front of City Hall?"

13 Then Janey's dad joined in. "Or maybe you're going to go door to door collecting signatures for a petition? What's your idea, dear? Don't keep us in the dark."

14 "Well", Janey's mom replied, "those are all excellent ideas, and I might try some of them later, if I need to. But I have another idea - I'm going to create a website about the speeding problem."

15 "Wow! A website! Mom, that's a great idea!" Janey exclaimed.

16 "Thanks, honey", said Janey's mom, laughing. "I just hope the community will be as excited about the website as you are!"

Questions

1. In paragraph 4, Janey's mom uses some figurative language. In the blank space below, write the figurative phrase, and then explain what it actually means.

____

____

2. Who is speaking in paragraph 5?

____

3. In paragraph 2, what does *exasperated* mean?
   a. very bored
   b. very happy
   c. very angry
   d. very hungry

4. What do we learn in paragraph 6 that helps us understand why Janey's mom was exasperated?

____

____

5. In paragraph 8, what does *ponder* mean?
   a. write a letter about
   b. think about
   c. talk about
   d. look up in a dictionary

6. What is Janey's mom's biggest concern about the speeding cars and trucks?

____

____

7. In paragraph 13, Janey's dad uses figurative language. In the blank space below, write the figurative phrase, and then explain what it actually means.

____

____

8. What is the main idea of this passage?
   a. speeding vehicles are dangerous
   b. nobody at City Hall cares about speeding vehicles
   c. discussing things at dinner is a good way to solve problems
   d. Janey's mom decides to make a website about the speeding vehicle problem

9. In paragraph 13, what does *petition* mean?
   a. a divider between two rooms
   b. a written request to someone in power
   c. a notebook
   d. a sign by the road

10. Do you agree with Janey's mom that the speed limit on the road by their house should be lowered? Answer Yes or No in the blank space below, and then give reasons for your answer.

____

____

Chapter 2: Mom Makes a List

1 Janey came in from riding her bike to get a drink of water and rest for a few minutes. She filled her glass and then sat down at the dining room table with her mom, who was writing in a notebook. "What are you writing about, Mom?" Janey inquired.

2 "I'm just making a few notes, dear. It's sort of a checklist of everything I need to do to get my new website up and running."

3 "Can I see your list?"

4 "Sure, Janey." Her mom smiled and handed her the notebook. "Let me know what you think."

5 Janey looked at her mom's list:

- Think of a website name.
- Think of a domain name.
- Buy the domain.
- Compare hosting plans.
- Buy hosting.
- Install blog software.

- Install forum software.
- Choose graphics, layout and design.

6 "Gosh, Mom! Hosting, graphics, blog, domain...I don't know what a lot of these words even mean."

7 Her mom laughed. "Don't worry about that stuff, dear. It's a lot of technical jargon. Until I started looking into how to create a website, I didn't know what some of those words meant, either."

8 "Boy oh boy, there's a lot more to making a website than I thought there was. It sounds really complicated."

9 "It does at first, doesn't it?" her mom replied. "Actually, though, it's really not very complicated at all. You just have to do a little research to make sure you've got all your ducks in a row."

10 "Well, Mom, I'm still glad you're the one who's doing it, and not me. I couldn't figure that stuff out in a million years."

11 Her mom laughed again. "A million? Ha! In just a few years you'll know so much about this stuff you'll be able to run circles around me!"

12 "You may be right, Mom. But right now I've got more important things to do, like riding my bike."

13 Janey and her mom both laughed as she grabbed her helmet and headed out the door.

Questions

1. In paragraph 1, what does *inquired* mean?
   a. whispered
   b. yelled
   c. asked
   d. told

2. Who is speaking in paragraph 8?

____

3. In paragraph 7, what does *jargon* mean?
   a. special words or phrases about a particular topic
   b. baby talk
   c. nonsense
   d. expensive tools

4. In paragraph 9, Janey's mom uses some figurative language. In the blank space below, write the figurative phrase, and then explain what it actually means.

____

____

5. Do you think Janey will help her mom make the website? Answer Yes or No, and then explain how you came up with your answer.

____

____

6. Divide the following words into syllables, like this: baseball base | ball

a. million _______________

b. domain _______________

c. technical _______________

d. hosting _______________

7. In paragraph 8, what does *complicated* mean?

a. easy to understand

b. difficult to understand

c. lots of fun

d. very boring

8. If someone read this passage, and he didn't know what *complicated* means, what are two sentences that would help him figure out what it means?

____

____

9. What kind of book can you use to find out what words mean?

____

____

10. Do you think you would enjoy creating your own website? Answer Yes or No, and give some reasons to explain your answer.

____

____

Chapter 3: Mom Launches Her Website

1 "Please pass the syrup, Dad," Janey said as she buttered her pancakes. She loved Saturday mornings. On Saturdays everybody slept in, and then the family always had pancakes for a late breakfast. "No alarm clock and pancakes make a great combination," thought Janey. There was something that was a little bit different this Saturday morning, though. At first, Janey couldn't quite put her finger on it. Then she suddenly realized what was different.

2 "*Mom!* That's got to be the fifth time you've yawned since we started breakfast. That's not like you at all. I'm the one who's usually yawning at the breakfast table."

3 Her mom started to reply, but then yawned again.

4 "Now, now, Janey, there's no need to reprimand your mother," Janey's dad said with a wink. "Don't worry; she's not turning into a night owl. She has a valid excuse for being tired. She was up until almost three in the morning putting the finishing touches on her website."

5 "Really, Mom? It's finally done and ready to go?"

6 "It sure is, Janey," her mom replied. "In fact, it's not just ready to go. It's actually 'on the air' right now. I published my first article right before I went to bed."

7 "Alright, Mom! Way to go!"

8 "Thanks, Janey, but this is only the beginning. There's still a lot of work to do. Let's not forget that the only reason I started this website is to get the speed limit on our street lowered to 35 miles an hour. The website is only a tool to help me accomplish that."

9 "I know, Mom, but it's still exciting, and I'm proud of you. I bet I'm the only one in my class whose mom has a website."

10 "Well, how would you like to help me with my website *and* be the star of your very own video on the internet?"

11 "That would be awesome, Mom!"

12 "I thought you might be interested," said Janey's mom, as she winked at Janey's dad. "Okay, then, we have a deal. We'll make the video next Friday after you get home from school. Of course, that's only if the weather is good, because we'll be making the video outside."

13 Janey was a bit disappointed. "Friday? Why can't we do it today, or Monday?"

14 "Well, we can't do it today because there's not as much traffic on Saturdays. I want the video to show people just how bad the problem is. And we can't do it on Monday, because you'll need time to memorize your script."

15 "I'm going to have a script? Really?"

16 "Yes, and I'm going to start writing it today, so you'll have all week to memorize it."

17 "Well, Mom and Dad, please excuse me from the breakfast table. If I'm going to be a movie star, I'd better start acting like one. If you need me, I'll be in my dressing room."

Questions

1. If Janey had to start going to school on Saturdays, do you think she would be happy or unhappy about it? Also, explain how you came up with your answer.

____

____

2. In paragraph 1, what does this sentence mean: "At first, Janey couldn't quite put her finger on it."

____

____

3. In paragraph 4, what does *reprimand* mean?
   a. ignore
   b. slap on the face
   c. stare at
   d. severely scold

4. Why does Janey's dad wink when he says there's no need to reprimand her mom?

____

____

5. Janey's dad is using figurative language when he tells Janey that her mom is not turning into a "night owl." What does "night owl" mean in that sentence?

____

____

6. In paragraph 4, what does *valid* mean?
   a. fake
   b. not true
   c. good
   d. sleepy

7. Who is speaking in paragraph 10?

____

8. Which word below does NOT have the same meaning as *accomplish* in paragraph 8?
   a. stop
   b. do
   c. achieve
   d. fulfill

9. Do you think the video will be more effective with lots of cars and trucks going by? Explain your answer.

____

____

10. Do you think Janey will work hard to memorize her script? Explain your answer.

____

____

Chapter 4: Lights! Camera! Janey!

1 Today was the big day - Janey was going be in a video for her mom's website. She had completely memorized her script by Tuesday, and she made it a point to rehearse her lines every night after school. Now Friday was finally here. Janey couldn't wait to get home and make the video. Normally she loved going to school, but today it seemed to drag on forever. Finally, the last bell of the day rang, and before she knew it the school bus was stopping in front of her house and dropping her off.

2 "Mom! I'm home!" Janey exclaimed as she opened the door and walked in. "Are we ready to start the video?"

3 Janey's mom was sitting at the kitchen table. "I'm in here, dear. Are you sure you're ready?"

4 "I sure am, Mom. I know every word of the script by heart."

5 "Okay, then. Let's make a video!"

6 They went outside to the front yard. Janey stood quietly while her mom looked for the best place for her to stand. "Alright, this looks like a great spot. If you stand here the viewers will be able to see you, and all the traffic."

7 Janey moved to the spot her mother had picked out. "Okay, Mom, I'm ready when you are."

8 "Okay, Janey. Stand there for a moment while I adjust the settings on the camera, and try not to fidget."

9 Janey stood as still as possible while her mom tried to get the distance and focus just right. Finally her mom was satisfied, and it was time to get started.

10 "When you see the red light on the camera come on, that will be your signal to start talking. You'll need to speak up, but don't yell. We've got plenty of time, so if you make a mistake, it's no big deal. We'll just start over. Now, look right into the camera, and when you see the red light, start talking."

11 Janey was nervous as she took a deep breath, and waited for the red light. There it was! She gave the camera a big smile, and started talking.

12 "Hi!. My name is Janey Peterson, and I'm making this video to alert the local community to a hazardous situation. I'm standing in the front yard of my house, which is located on Old Mill Road. My family and I love living here, except for one thing. The speed limit is too high, and it's making things dangerous. We moved here five years ago and there were hardly any other houses out here, and there was very little traffic. Having a 55 mile per hour speed limit wasn't a problem then. Things have changed, however. Since then, lots of families have built houses on Old Mill Road, and several factories have been built a few miles from here. Hundreds of people work in these factories, and a lot of them use our road for a shortcut. So do many other people. As you can see, one car after another is speeding down the road right behind me. This goes on constantly, and it's very dangerous. If something isn't done, it's only a matter of time before someone is injured. My mom has called, emailed and visited City Hall to try to get the speed limit lowered, but nothing has been done. So we're asking for your help. Please contact the folks at City Hall and ask them to lower the speed limit on Old Mill Road to 35 miles per hour before someone gets hurt. Thank you."

13 "That was great, Janey!"

14 "Was it really that good, Mom?" Janey asked

15 "It sure was!"

16 "Do you want me to do it again? I don't mind."

17 "No, Janey, that won't be necessary. You did a great job. Now let's go put this video on my website."

Questions

1. In paragraph 1, what does *rehearse* mean?
   a. write down
   b. say into a recorder
   c. practice
   d. forget

2. Who is speaking in paragraph 5?

____

3. What is another word that means the same thing as *hazardous* in paragraph 12?

____

____

4. In paragraph 8, Janey's mom asks her to try not to *fidget*. What word below has the same meaning as *fidget*?
   a. giggle
   b. squirm
   c. whisper
   d. blink

5. When Janey was at school, why do you think she felt like the day seemed to "drag on forever"?

____

____

6. Which of these words would NOT be a good replacement for *satisfied* in paragraph 9?
   a. happy
   b. content
   c. pleased
   d. upset

7. Janey did an excellent job in the video. Most people giving a speech in front of a camera would make one or more mistakes, and would have to do it over several times. Why do you think Janey did a great job on her first try?

____

____

8. Which word or phrase would NOT be a good replacement for *constantly* in paragraph 12?
   a. rarely
   b. all the time
   c. regularly
   d. continually

9. Janey and her mom want the speed limit on Old Mill Road lowered to 35 miles per hour. Do you think making this video will help them achieve their goal? Answer Yes or No, and give some reasons for your answer.

____

____

10. What is the main idea of this chapter?
   a. school is boring
   b. it's hard to find a good spot for making a video
   c. Janey makes her video for her mom's website
   d. practice makes perfect

Chapter 5: A Team Effort

1 The activity on Janey's mom's cellphone was ceaseless. All day long she had been receiving calls from friends and neighbors who wanted to congratulate her for being successful at getting the speed limit lowered. Her idea to start a website about the problem had really paid off, and this morning every home on Old Mill Road had received an official letter from the city. The letter was letting them know that in the next few weeks city workers would be putting up signs with the new speed limit: 35 miles per hour.

2 "Gosh, Mom! You're a hero!" Janey exclaimed after her mom finally turned off her phone.

3 "Not really, Janey. I'm just someone who spoke up about a problem that needed to be solved, and I'm only one person. It was all of our neighbors who contacted City Hall about the problem who made the difference. When it was just one person complaining, the city leaders felt like they could ignore me. But they couldn't ignore several dozen people calling and writing. That's what made the difference, not me. Alone, one individual

usually can't accomplish much, but when numerous people take action, things change."

4 "Well, Mom, none of that would have happened if you hadn't made the website. People started reading it, and emailing their friends and neighbors, and then they all came to the big meeting you and Dad organized and announced on the website. They took action, but you're the one who helped persuade them to take action. Admit it, Mom - you made it happen! I'm proud of you!"

5 "Well, I guess I can take a little bit of credit," Mom said, "but let's not forget your contribution. The video you made really helped people understand that children are in danger from these cars zooming past our houses. Many people told me that watching your video is what motivated them to get involved."

6 "So it was a team effort, Mom?"

7 "It certainly was, Janey. You played a big part, and you should be proud of yourself. Your father and I are certainly proud of you."

8 "Thank you, Mom!"

9 "You're very welcome, dear. And I know another team effort you can help me with."

8 "What's that, Mom?"

9 "Eating the pizza your father is picking up on the way home to celebrate our victory."

10 "Eating pizza? That kind of team effort is right up my alley!"

Questions

1. Which word below would NOT be a good replacement for *ceaseless* in paragraph 1?
   a. never-ending
   b. continuous
   c. extremely loud
   d. non-stop

2. The two items below share a cause and effect relationship. Label each as either CAUSE or EFFECT.

People call city hall to ask that the speed limit be lowered.

____

Janey makes a video about the speeding vehicle problem.

____

3. In your opinion, who played a more important part in getting the speed limit changed - Janey, or her mom? Give reasons for your answer.

____

____

4. List two words from paragraph 1 that have four syllables.

____

____

5. Which word would NOT be a good substitute for *contribution* in paragraph 5?
   a. share
   b. part
   c. help
   d. name

6. Janey tells her mom that if she hadn't made the website, the speeding problem would not been solved. Do you agree with Janey? Why or why not?

____

____

7. What word in paragraph 4 means to convince someone to believe something or do something?

____

8. In paragraph 10, Janey says eating pizza is *right up my alley*. What does she mean?

____

____

9. What word in paragraph 1 means to praise someone for something they accomplished?

____

10. Janey's mom says that getting the speed limit lowered was a team effort. Besides Janey and her mom, who else was part of the team?

____

____

The Big Picture Quiz

Answer the following questions using the information in all five story chapters. When answering, just use the chapter number, not the title.

1. In which chapter did Janey have trouble concentrating in school?

____

2. Name at least three things Janey likes.

____

3. In which chapter did Janey's mom have trouble staying awake at the breakfast table?

____

4. In which chapter did Janey's mom have to shut off her cell phone because it wouldn't quit ringing?

____

5. Name two foods that Janey likes a lot.

____

6. Before she made her website, how had Janey's mom tried to persuade the officials at City Hall to lower the speed limit?

____

7. Have you learned any new words from this story? If so, write them below.

____

____

8. What do you think of Janey's mom's efforts to get the speed limit reduced? Do you think it was a good idea? Can you think of any ideas that might have been better?

____

____

____

9. What street does Janey's family live on?

____

10. Can you think of anything in your neighborhood that needs to be improved or changed? Explain, and then write about what you might be able to do to help make things different.

____

____

____

In China, New Year's Day is a day for great celebrations. People have big parades, and some of them dress up like a monster called Nian. Almost every family glues red paper to their front doors, keeps the lights on in every room of the house until after midnight, and lights fireworks. This Chinese folk tale explains why they do these things.

How Nian Was Defeated

Chinese New Year Lion Dance Costume

1 Once upon a time, near the village of Taohun (Peach Blossom), there lived a huge beast at the bottom of the sea. His name was Nian, and once a year, on New Year's Day, he would come forth out of the sea for one day. After spending all year at the bottom of the ocean, Nian was very hungry. He would eat just about everything he could see. He ate the crops, and he ate the cows, pigs and horses. He ate pets, too. He still wasn't satisfied, though, so he would even eat human beings. Nian especially loved to eat children. If he couldn't find anything to eat, he would get so angry he would destroy everything in his path.

2 The people who lived in Taohun were very afraid of Nian. So on New Year's Eve, the day before Nian's arrival, they would flee the village so he wouldn't eat them. The entire village would head to the top of the faraway mountains so that Nian couldn't find them. If they had animals, they would try to take them with them. Every year, though, Nian managed to catch and eat some of the slowest villagers. All year long the villagers lived in dread, knowing that Nian would come out of the ocean on New Year's Day. Even if they managed to avoid being eaten, when they came back to the village they would have to rebuild everything Nian had destroyed.

3 One year an old beggar wandered into the village on New Year's Eve. He went from house to house asking for a bite to eat, but everyone ignored him. They were terrified of the monster, and they were hurrying as fast as they could to get ready to flee the village. Finally an old lady who lived right by the ocean felt sorry for the beggar. She gave him a bite to eat, but then warned him to flee. "Don't you know what day it is tomorrow? Get to the mountains before Nian eats you!"

4 But the old beggar wasn't scared. Instead, he smiled mysteriously. When the woman asked him how he could smile at a time like this, he simply replied, "Ma'am, if you will shelter me in your house for one evening, I will see to it that Nian never terrorizes the village again." The old woman looked at him like he was crazy. Before long it would be dark, and there wasn't much time to spare. "Look, you can't stay in my house. Nian will be coming soon, so you must flee for your life!" But the old man didn't say anything; he just kept smiling mysteriously. Finally the woman decided that there was no more time to argue with him, and she shook her head sadly as she walked out of the house and headed for the mountains. There was nothing more she could do. If the old beggar was foolish enough to stay in her house, he would be sorry.

5 Soon enough, everyone in the village was gone, except for the old beggar in the house. They had all fled to the mountains for safety. At one second past midnight, Nian rose from the bottom of the ocean, just as he did every year. The first house he came to was the old lady's, and he prepared to knock it down in search of something to eat. But just as he started to run toward the door, he noticed something was different this year. There was red paper glued to the door. He was scared of the color red. The house was lit up in every room, and that frightened him even more. Then fireworks started going off, which terrified him. Quivering like a leaf, Nian tucked his tail between his legs and ran back into the ocean.

6 The next day all the people of the village came home. They were shocked to discover that there was no damage to the village at all. They were puzzled and happy at the same time, and they all began to ask each other why Nian hadn't destroyed the village this year. The old lady told them

about the strange beggar, and the promise he had made to her. Filled with curiosity and excitement, everyone ran over to the old lady's house. They saw the red paper on the door, all the candles burning in the house, and the used fireworks in the yard. They wondered what it could mean. Then the old beggar came out of the house and explained to them that Nian was afraid of lights, the color red, and loud noises. After that, every year on New Year's Eve, the people of Peach Blossom glued red paper to their doors, lit candles in every room, and set off fireworks to keep Nian away, and he never troubled them again.

Questions

1. In paragraph 1, which word means the same thing as *sea*?

2. Is this story true?

3. In which country do you think Peach Blossom is located? How did you decide that?

4. Why was the old beggar smiling mysteriously?

5. In paragraph 5, what does *quivering* mean?

6. What does *Taohun* mean in English? How do you know?

7. In paragraph 2, what does *dread* mean?

____

8. What is the central lesson of this story?

____

9. Which of these books does this story have the most in common with?
   a. *The Story of George Washington*
   b. *The History of the United States*
   c. *The Legend of Paul Bunyan*
   d. *How to Play Baseball*

10. Do you think the beggar had any trouble getting the people of Taohun to give him food after what happened? Explain your answer.

____

____

Reading: Informational Texts

Our Neighbor Mercury

1 Earth is a planet with many neighbors. Besides Earth, there are seven other full sized planets in the solar system, and the one that is the closest to the sun is named Mercury. Earth is about two and a half times the size of Mercury. The surface of Mercury is very rough, like our moon. There are lots of craters, and it is completely barren, with nothing but soil as far as the eye can see. Do you know how Mercury got its name? The name comes from ancient Rome, some 24 centuries ago. The Romans believed in many different gods, and the messenger of the gods was called Mercury. He was able to move extremely fast. Because this planet moves around the sun faster than any other planets, it was given the name Mercury.

2 Sometimes Mercury is closer to our planet than at other times, but it is always a long way away. The closest it ever gets to us is about 40 million miles. It is much closer to the sun than Earth is, so it doesn't take it nearly as long to revolve around the sun. In fact, it only takes 88 days for Mercury to orbit the sun. So, here on earth a year is 365 days long, but on Mercury a year is only 88 days long. So, if you're 10 years old, if you lived on Mercury you would be almost 42 years old!

3 If that's not strange enough, consider this. Earth orbits around the sun, and it also rotates, like a spinning top. One full rotation is 24 hours, or one day. Well, Mercury also rotates, but much more slowly. A day on Mercury is 58 Earth days. Since a year on Mercury is only 88 Earth days, that means there are only one and a half "days" in a Mercury year. That would be like the sun coming up on Earth and then it would be sunny 24 hours a day for four months, and then it would be dark for four months straight, and then sunny again for four months. That would be very hard to get used to. So living on Mercury with a day that is actually 58 Earth days long would be quite a change.

4 Of course, there's no chance that anyone will ever actually live on Mercury. It's impossible, because of the temperatures on the planet. Temperatures can range from 300 degrees below zero to around 800 degrees. 800 degrees is hot enough to melt some metals. We would broil to death almost instantly on Mercury. When it got dark, we would freeze to death. Some people believe that one of these days an astronaut will walk on Mars, but that will never happen on Mercury!

Questions

1. Using the information you learned in this article, find Mercury on this map and circle it. (The big item on the left is the Sun, and Earth is the third planet away from the sun.)

http://open.nasa.gov/wp-content/uploads/2011/04/solarsys_scale.jpg2

2. One of the planets below is Earth, and the other planet is Mercury. Which one is Earth?
   a. the planet on the left
   b. the planet on the right

3. What is the main reason people could never visit Mercury, or live there?

____

4. Which planet has a longer year, Mercury or Earth?

____

5. What kind of story is this?
   a. entertaining
   b. informational

6. What is the main purpose of this story?
   a. to explain how long a year is
   b. to discuss the entire solar system
   c. to give facts about the sun
   d. to give facts about the planet Mercury

7. What is the closest Mercury ever comes to earth?
   a. about 40 million miles
   b. about 400 miles
   c. about 400 million miles
   d. about 4 miles

8. What word in paragraph 1 means huge holes?

____

9. What word below means the same thing as *barren* in paragraph 1?
   a. blue
   b. round
   c. lifeless
   d. gigantic

10. Write three things a person can learn about the planet Mercury by reading this story.

____

____

____

11. In paragraph 1, what does *ancient* mean, and what clue can a person use to figure out what it means if they've never seen the word before?

____

____

12. In paragraph 2, what word means the same thing as *revolve*?

____

13. Why do you think it gets so much hotter on Mercury than on Earth?

____

14. Why does the story call Mercury our neighbor?

____

15. Mercury is some 40 million miles away from Earth. If someone lived 40 miles from your house, would they be your neighbor? Why or why not?

____

Montana: Big Sky Country

Glacier National Park, Montana

[1] Most people know that Alaska is the biggest state. Many people know that Texas is 2nd, and California is 3rd . Lots of people know the top three, but do you know which state is 4th when it comes to size? It's Montana. (It's also the biggest state that doesn't border a large body of water.)

[2] This massive state (over 147,000 square miles) is located in the northwest area of the US. It became the 41st state when it was admitted to the Union on November 8, 1889. Montana is bordered by four states - North Dakota, South Dakota, Wyoming, and Idaho. It is also bordered by another country, Canada.

[3] Many people believe that Montana is one of the most scenic states. It certainly does have a lot of natural beauty. Its name means "mountain" in Spanish, and there are certainly lots of mountains there. Most mountains are on the western side of the state; the rest of the state is basically flat. Montana also contains many national and state parks. Part of Yellowstone National Park, one of the most famous natural attractions in the world, is in Montana. The state is also full of wildlife not found in most states, such as bighorn sheep, mountain lions, mountain goats, elk, bobcats, lynx, bison, black bears, and grizzly bears, to name just a few.

[4] Montana has several nicknames. One of them is "Big Sky Country", and another is "The Treasure State." The latter nickname refers to the fact that mining used to be a big industry in Montana, and that many people came to the area back in the 1800s searching for gold. These days, farming is the

Bighorn Sheep in Montana

most common business in the state. Farmers in Montana raise lots of wheat, hay, barley and other crops. There are over two and a half million head of cattle in the state, and hundreds of thousands of sheep.

5 One of the most famous battles in American history took place in Montana. It's officially known as Battle of the Little Bighorn, but many people call it Custer's Last Stand. Many Native Americans call it the Battle of the Greasy Grass. It took place in 1876, when Montana was still part of a territory, and not a state yet. It was a battle between the US Army and two Native American tribes, the Lakota and the Cheyenne. The battle has become legendary because the Native Americans outnumbered the Army, and defeated them badly. General George Custer and almost 300 soldiers died on the battlefield. The battlefield is now a national monument. So Montana is not only full of beauty and natural resources, but it's also rich in history.

Questions

1. In paragraph 1, what word means *to be next to*?

____

2. In paragraph 2, what does *massive* mean?

____

3. In paragraph 4, what does *latter* mean?
   a. first
   b. something you climb on to reach something higher
   c. the second of two
   d. largest

4. Which of these would be biggest?
   a. a large statue
   b. a big statue
   c. a sizable statue
   d. a gigantic statue

5. Where would you find most of the mountains in Montana?

____

6. Part of one of the most famous natural attractions in the world is in Montana. What is its name?

____

7. Who fought Native Americans at the Battle of the Little Bighorn?

____

8. In paragraph 3, what does *scenic* mean?
   a. having natural beauty
   b. gigantic
   c. foul smelling
   d. rainy

9. In paragraph 5, what word means *very famous*?

____

10. If you had to choose another title for this article, which of these would be best?
   a. Let's Explore Montana
   b. Montana's Biggest Mountain
   c. The Montana Gold Rush
   d. Why People Don't Like Montana

11. In paragraph 1, is *border* a noun or a verb?

____

12. List five things about Montana that might make people want to visit the state.

____

____

Linda Richards, Medical Pioneer

Linda Richards

1 All Americans should be thankful for Linda Richards. Who was she? Well, let me explain. Just about everyone has been to the doctor, and many of us have had to spend some time in a hospital. Most of us don't like going to the doctor's office, and nobody looks forward to going to the hospital. It's no fun to be sick, get shots, have tests, or be confined to a bed.

2 However, there are people whose job it is to take care of us while we're being treated by doctors. They are called nurses, and they have helped hundreds of millions of Americans feel better and get well faster over the years. All of us should be grateful for nurses, because nearly all of us have been helped by a nurse at one time or another, and we all have several family members who have been brought back to health thanks to the efforts of nurses. Well, Linda Richards is one of the "Founding Mothers" of modern nursing.

3 Linda Richards was born in West Potsdam, New York, in 1841. Her father was a preacher, and he wanted Linda to become a missionary after she grew up. However, her father died when she was only four years old. Then her mother became very sick, and Linda spent years taking care of her mother until she died when Linda was fourteen. A lot of people would feel sorry for themselves if both their parents died when they were young, and they might never get over it. Linda Richards was different, though. She had enjoyed taking care of her mother, and she decided that she was going to become a nurse, and not a missionary.

4 Linda Richards wasn't the first nurse in the world by any stretch of the imagination. Nurses have been around for centuries, but until recently, nursing was a lot different than it is today. Back in the old days, most nurses weren't very educated. Some of them couldn't read or write, and they knew little about medicine or health. They mostly did things to make patients feel

more comfortable, such as give them a drink of water, help them go to the bathroom, or wipe their foreheads with a wet rag. These tasks are very important, but there is a lot more a nurse needs to know and do to help people get well. Linda Richards understood that, and she helped change nursing into the modern profession it is today.

5 After helping a local doctor for a while, she took a nursing job at a hospital in Boston, but it was an awful experience. There was no training, and nurses were expected to work from 6 in the morning to 9:30 at night. They also had to sleep at the hospital, near their patients, and would have to get up every time a patient called them. This was very hard on nurses, and many of them quit. Linda was one of them, and she soon became a student in the first class ever held at America's very first nursing school. After she graduated, she became a supervisor at Bellevue Hospital in New York City. While she worked there, she invented a way of keeping records for each patient. It might sound hard to believe, but until Linda Richards came along, most hospitals didn't keep very good track of their patients and their health. She changed all that, and before long all hospitals in America were keeping patient records.

6 She didn't stop there. Linda Richards kept getting more education for herself. She even went to England to study with Florence Nightingale, the most famous nurse in history. After she returned to America, she began starting nursing schools across the country in order to train people in the modern methods of nursing. Pretty soon, nurses who had an education in health and medicine were helping patients all over America. Linda Richards did more than anyone else has ever done to improve nursing in America, and thanks to her, millions of people have lived longer and better lives.

Florence Nightingale

Questions

1. Which of these words has the same meaning as *pioneer*?
   a. follower
   b. trailblazer
   c. English
   d. doctor

2. In paragraph 1, what does *confined* mean?
   a. under
   b. opposed to
   c. on top of
   d. stuck in

3. Which of these helped Linda Richards decide to become a nurse?
   a. coming down with the flu
   b. seeing a vision from God
   c. taking care of her sick mother
   d. her pet cat dying

4. In paragraph 4, which word means *hundreds of years*?

____

5. Choose the sentence below which has the same meaning as: *Linda Richards wasn't the first nurse in the world by any stretch of the imagination.*
   a. Linda Richards was far from being the first nurse in the world.
   b. Linda Richards was almost the first nurse in the world.
   c. Linda Richards was basically the first nurse who ever lived.
   d. Linda Richards was one of the first nurses in the world.

6. Do you think Linda Richards had a computer in her house? Explain your answer.

___

7. Which of these is NOT something Linda Richards did?
   a. created a system of keeping records for hospital patients
   b. discovered a new medicine
   c. attended the first nursing school in America
   d. founded several nursing schools

8. What would be the best word to describe the working conditions Linda Richards experienced at her first hospital job in Boston?
   a. pleasant
   b. enjoyable
   c. brutal
   d. fun

9. Put the following events from Linda Richards' life in order, writing 1, 2, 3, or 4 beside each one
   a. She went to England to study with Florence Nightingale
   b. She took care of her dying mother
   c. She invented a record keeping system
   d. She took a job at Bellevue Hospital

10. What word in paragraph 6 means *make better*?

___

Becoming a Teacher

1 Have you ever wondered how a person becomes a teacher? It isn't easy. First you have to graduate from high school, and do so with good grades. You need to have good grades so you can go to college. Colleges aren't like elementary school, or high school - they can choose the students they want, and reject students they don't want. You have to apply to go to colleges, and the colleges can either accept you as a student, or turn you down. It's their decision. Well, colleges like to have smart students, so a person with good high school grades will have a better chance of going to college. So, if you want to be a teacher someday, make sure you get good grades!

2 Once you have been accepted into college, that's only the beginning. You might have to pass another test to even be allowed to study to become a teacher. If you don't pass it, you will have to study for another career. Then you must go to school and study hard for several years. Many people earn a college degree in four years, but for lots of people it can take six or more years. That's a long time - imagine yourself six years from now. You'll be in 9th grade! It's also a lot of hard work and studying. Future teachers have to study many subjects, like math and English, but they also have to study how to teach different subjects. Teaching kids how to do math is a lot different than teaching them science. There is a lot to learn if you want to become a teacher.

3 Well, after you've studied hard and graduated from college after several years of hard work, guess what? You have to take some more tests. That's right; if you want to be a teacher, finishing college doesn't mean you're done with taking tests. When schools hire a teacher, they want to be

completely sure the teacher is well educated, and can do a good job of teaching students. So, even though you already have a degree, you will have to take some more tests. If you pass them, then you will be given a teaching license, and you can start applying for schoolteacher jobs. That may not be the last test you'll have to take, though. In many states, every few years teachers have to take a test to make sure they're still doing a good job. If they fail, they will lose their teaching job. So, if you want to be a teacher, you had better get used to taking tests. And you probably thought taking tests was for students, not for teachers! Don't worry, though. If you really want to become a teacher, and you pay attention and study hard, you can do it. Just realize that becoming a teacher is not a piece of cake!

Questions

1. What would be a good word or phrase to replace *wondered* in paragraph 1?
    a. decided
    b. considered
    c. talked about
    d. wrote a letter about

2. What is another way of saying colleges can turn you down?
    a. colleges can turn you in
    b. colleges can reject you
    c. colleges can accept you
    d. colleges can invite you

3. According to this article, can a person become a teacher without going to college?

____

4. Which sentence in paragraph 3 contains figurative language?

____

5. What does the author mean when he says *becoming a teacher is not a piece of cake*?

____

Polar Bears

Polar Bear

1 Polar bears are fascinating creatures. Did you know that they are among the biggest bears in the world? It's true; they're even bigger than grizzly bears. A male polar bear can weigh anywhere from 800 to 1500 pounds, and will be between eight and ten feet long. Here's another fact about polar bears that many people don't know: they spend much of their time in or on the water. In fact, their scientific name is *Ursus maritimus*, which is Latin for "bear of the sea." They are born on land, and they do spend a lot of time on land, but they spend much of their time in the water (or on the ice on top of the water) because their main food source is seals.

2 Polar bears are only found in areas around the North Pole, and in only five countries: Norway, Canada, Russia, Greenland and the United States (only in Alaska). Their fur is white, which helps them blend in with the snow. This makes it easier to sneak up on seals and catch them, because it's hard for the seals to see them. They also have long snouts and long necks; these help them to look down into holes in the ice over the sea so they can catch seals underwater. Their thick fur allows them to live in an area with very cold temperatures, and their strong claws and teeth are ideal for catching and eating their food. They also have very wide feet. Their big feet and claws allow them to walk on ice without slipping.

Polar Bear Cubs

3 Baby polar bears are born in the winter, between November and February. It's hard to believe how tiny they are at birth. They only weigh about 2 pounds. They are also blind when they're born; their sight develops after they're born. Young polar bears are called cubs. Usually a mother will have two cubs at the same time. They will stay with their mother for around two years before they go out on their own. Most polar bears live for about 20 years.

4 Right now there are about 25,000 polar bears in the world. That might sound like a lot, but it really isn't. Many experts believe that this number is getting smaller every year. Some people are worried that polar bears are going to disappear forever, or go extinct, like wooly mammoths and saber-toothed tigers did. They say that the amount of ice at the North Pole is getting smaller every year. Polar bears need ice in order to survive. Will polar bears go extinct? Let's hope not. Scientists are working hard to prevent this, and we all hope they succeed.

Questions

1. Are there polar bears in Mexico? Explain your answer.

____

2. In paragraph 1, what does *fascinating* mean?
    a. moving at high speed
    b. very interesting
    c. not popular
    d. four-legged

3. What is the polar bear's scientific name?

____

4. Why are there no more wooly mammoths or saber-toothed tigers?

____

5. List at least three things about polar bears that help them survive in snow and ice.

____

6. Is Smoky Bear a polar bear? Explain your answer.

____

7. If you found a polar bear which was six months old, would you expect its mother to be nearby? Explain your answer.

8. In paragraph 4, what does succeed mean?

Walruses

Walrus

1 What is the funniest looking animal on earth? Well, there are a lot of funny looking animals in the world, but without a doubt, one of the funniest looking ones is the walrus. They look funny when they're sitting around, they look funny when they're lying down, and they really look funny when they pull themselves out of the water or across the ice by using their long tusks to help them move. In fact, walruses are so funny looking that they're cute! Here's something I bet you didn't know about walruses. Their scientific name is *Odobenus*. That's Latin for "toothwalker."

2 Besides being funny looking, walruses are also huge. They are between eight and twelve feet long, and can weigh nearly 4,000 pounds. They look like gargantuan balls of blubber with two gigantic teeth! In fact, they really are gargantuan balls of blubber - under their skin is a layer of fat that is almost six inches thick. This fat layer is like having a very thick swimsuit on; it keeps them warm in the extremely frigid water where they obtain their food. Their whiskers also contribute to their funny appearance, but they also serve a very important purpose - they help the walrus find its food. Their tusks are around three feet long, and are used for breaking ice, climbing out of the water, and for fighting.

Walrus Whiskers

3 When they're young, walruses have brown skin. It turns lighter and lighter as they age, and the older ones look almost pink. They usually live to be around 25 years old, but some can be as old as 30. Their main foods are small sea creatures such as shrimp, crabs and clam, which they find on the bottom of the sea. They use their whiskers to feel around for food on the sea floor, and they will force creatures out of hiding by spraying a mouthful of water in their direction. They can stay under water for long periods before coming up for air. They can also float for hours at the surface, because they have air bags under their throats.

4 There aren't many animals that eat walruses, which is a good thing, because they are so big they can't move fast enough to get away from a predator. Polar bears and killer whales will attack walruses, but usually they eat young or injured ones. An adult walrus can fight back hard, so killer whales and polar bears prefer to avoid them if they can. All in all, walruses have a pretty sweet life. They get to spend their days swimming in the ocean or lying in the sun, they have all the food they want for free, and the only things they really have to worry about are killer whales and polar bears. Most animals would love to have such an easy life. So walruses might be funny looking, but they're the ones who have the last laugh!

Questions

1. What clue in paragraph 1 helps a reader understand why walruses are also called toothwalkers?

____

2. The author says that walruses are one of the funniest looking animals on earth. Is this a fact, or an opinion?

____

3. What does *gargantuan* mean in paragraph 2?

____

4. What clue or clues would help a person figure out the meaning of *gargantuan*?

____

5. If there weren't enough clues to show the meaning of *gargantuan*, where would a person look to find the meaning?

____

6. In paragraph 3, is *age* a noun or a verb?

____

7. What does *age* mean in that paragraph?

____

8. In paragraph 4, what does *predator* mean?

____

9. What context clues can help the readers understand what *predator* means if they don't know the word?

10. Which part of the walrus helps it find food on the bottom of the sea?

____

Levi Coffin: President of the Underground Railroad

Levi Coffin

1 Fountain City is a very small town in eastern Indiana. Only about 800 people live in there, but every year, during the third weekend of September, people from all over come to visit Fountain City for the Levi Coffin Days festival. Levi Coffin lived there from 1826 to 1847, and he used his house to hide runaway slaves, and he also helped them get to Canada where they would be free. There were other people back then who also used their houses to hide runaway slaves. Together, these houses were called the Underground Railroad. Levi Coffin helped so many slaves escape that he became known as the President of the Underground Railroad.

2 Levi Coffin was born to a Quaker family in North Carolina in 1798. Slavery was legal then, but Quakers were a religious group who disapproved of it. When he was growing up, Levi met many slaves and would often talk to them. He felt sorry for them, and this helped turn him into an abolitionist. An abolitionist was a person who not only disapproved of slavery, but worked to have it outlawed. Many abolitionists also made efforts to help slaves escape. This was against the law, and a person could get into big trouble for helping runaway slaves. Slaves were considered property, and so helping them escape was considered to be stealing from their owner. It also violated the Fugitive Slave Act, which required people to return runaway slaves to their owners. There were people called slave catchers who were paid to capture runaway slaves and bring them back to their owners, and some of them would beat people up for helping slaves escape. So helping slaves escape was not only illegal, but dangerous.

3 Levi Coffin knew that helping slaves escape was illegal and dangerous, but he did it anyway. He hated slavery and wanted to end it. In fact, he hated it so much that he and his wife moved to Indiana, because slavery was illegal there. Back then Fountain City was called Newport, and Levi and his wife bought a farm and opened a general store there. His store was successful, and he began using the money he was making to help runaway slaves. He let other abolitionists know that slaves were welcome to stay at his house. He built secret rooms in his home where they could hide if a slave catcher showed up looking for them. Then at night he would put them in his wagon, cover them up, and take the slaves to the next house on the Underground Railroad.

Levi Coffin House

4 Levi Coffin helped more slaves escape than anyone else - over 2,000 slaves spent time in his home over the years. In 1865, after the Civil War, slavery was outlawed in the United States. Levi Coffin died in 1877, so he lived long enough to see his goal of ending slavery fulfilled. Now the house where he hid 2,000 runaway slaves is a National Historic Landmark, and every September, people come to Fountain City to celebrate his life.

Questions

1. Did Levi Coffin grow up in a family that owned slaves? Explain your answer.

____

____

2. Is this sentence a fact, or an opinion? *Slaves were considered property, and so helping them escape was considered to be stealing from their owner.*

____

3. Why did Levi Coffin move to Indiana?

____

4. According to this article, was slavery legal in Canada? Explain your answer.

____

5. Which of the words below means the same thing as *fulfilled* in paragraph 4?
   a. destroyed
   b. denied
   c. ended
   d. accomplished

6. In paragraph 2, what is a word that means the same thing as *runaway*?

____

7. What word in paragraph 3 means *against the law*?

____

8. The word that means *against the law* in paragraph 3 was made by adding a prefix to a base word. What is the base word, and what is the prefix?

____

9. Put these events in order of when they took place, by numbering them 1, 2, 3, and 4.

a. the Civil War _____

b. Levi Coffin died _____

c. the Underground Railroad started _____

d. slavery was outlawed _____

10. What is the old name for Fountain City?

____

One Giant Leap for Mankind

Neil Armstrong

1 On July 20, 1969, Neil Armstrong became the first man to walk on the moon, as 500 million people around the world watched on television. This was truly a historic event. Almost all people throughout history would have laughed at the idea that one day a man would walk on the moon. They would have said it was impossible. They would have called a person "crazy" for even talking about the idea. But on July 20, 1969 the man from a small Ohio town proved them wrong.

2 Neil Armstrong was born on August 5, 1930, in Wapakoneta, Ohio. His father had to travel for his job, so the Armstrong family moved about 20 times while Neil was a boy. They moved back to Wapakoneta permanently when he was 14. By this time Neil was in love with flying. Airplanes were still new back then, and most people had never been in one, but Neil took his first plane ride when he was only six years old. He fell in love with flying, and when he was a teenager he started taking flying lessons. He even got a license to fly even before he was old enough to get a driver's license! He was also active in Boy Scouting, and earned its highest rank of Eagle Scout.

3 Neil went off to college at Purdue University in Indiana right after he turned 17. He studied for two years, and then served in the Navy, where he became a fighter pilot. He fought in the Korean War, and then came back

to finish his college degree. After college, he joined the Air Force and became a pilot who tested new kinds of aircraft. During his career, he flew in over 200 different kinds of vehicles. It was during this time that the government created NASA to explore space, and in 1962 Neil Armstrong was selected to train as an astronaut.

4 In 1961, President John F. Kennedy had announced that he wanted NASA to land on the moon before 1970. That meant Neil Armstrong and the other astronauts had to work hard to get ready. The work was very dangerous, and some men died while exploring space. Neil Armstrong and the other astronauts bravely continued, though, and Neil was selected to be the first human being to set foot on the moon. After they returned to Earth, he and the other astronauts became national heroes. Neil Armstrong could have used his fame to make a lot of money or run for president, but instead he chose to live a quiet life out of the spotlight, and so he became a college professor. He didn't go on TV or give interviews very often, and he didn't like traveling around giving speeches. He died on August 25, 2012, at age 82. Many people lead remarkable lives, but Neil Armstrong's life was truly "out of this world."

First Man on the Moon

Questions

1. When did President Kennedy announce the goal of going to the moon by 1970?

___

2. Why was it a historic event when Neil Armstrong walked on the moon?

___

3. What did Neil Armstrong do in between starting and finishing his college degree at Purdue?

___

4. In paragraph 4, what is the root word of *bravely*?

___

5. Which phrase below means the same thing as *permanently* in paragraph 2?

   a. on time
   b. before dark
   c. for good
   d. at the same time

6. Is Wapakoneta a big city or a small town? Explain your answer.

___

7. In paragraph four, what phrase means "not attracting much attention"?

___

8. In paragraph 4, when the author says Neil Armstrong's life was truly *out of this world,* this is a play on words. It has two different meanings. What are they?

Phonics and Word Recognition

Prefixes and Suffixes

Prefixes

Prefixes are parts of words that are attached to the beginning of root words, which change the meaning of the root word. Take the word *do*, for example. If you add *re-* to *do*, you get *redo*, which means do something again." If your clock is wrong, and you need to set it again, you *reset* it. *Pre-* is also a prefix, which means "before." *Post-* is a prefix which means "after." *Un-* can mean "not", or "opposite." If your friend is not happy, he is *unhappy*. If your neighbor is the opposite of friendly, she is *unfriendly*. *Mis-* means "wrong", so if you aren't paying attention, you might *miscount* the money from your piggy bank. There are lots of different prefixes, but many of them aren't very common. Here is an exercise to help you with some of the prefixes you will see on a regular basis.

For each problem, fill in the blank with the correct answer.

1. If you don't respect someone, you ____________ him.
   a. unrespect
   b. prerespect
   c. misrespect
   d. disrespect

2. My neighbor mumbles a lot, so I sometimes ______________ her.
   a. ununderstand
   b. disunderstand
   c. misunderstand
   d. reunderstand

3. Oh, no! The rain washed our sandcastle away, so we will have to __________ it.
   a. rebuild
   b. postbuild
   c. prebuild
   d. unbuild

4. That boy is very silly; almost everything he says is ______________.
   a. unsense
   b. nonsense
   c. postsense
   d. dissense

5. We will have to ______________ the frozen turkey before we cook it.
   a. refrost
   b. unfrost
   c. defrost
   d. disfrost

6. It's ___________ for a person to run faster than a horse.
   a. nonpossible
   b. unpossible
   c. impossible
   d. depossible

7. Something that doesn't happen very often is ____________.
   a. infrequent
   b. subfrequent
   c. bifrequent
   d. overfrequent

8. I don't enjoy cold weather so I ____________ winter.
   a. inlike
   b. dislike
   c. unlike
   d. relike

9. Do you agree or ____________?
   a. unagree
   b. disagree
   c. misagree
   d. imagree

10. If your answer was wrong, ____________ the problem and try again.
   a. overthink
   b. unthink
   c. disthink
   d. rethink

11. It's ____________ to drive fast in a schoolzone.
   a. unsafe
   b. imsafe
   c. desafe
   d. undersafe

12. The sign says it's ____________ to park here.
   a. prelegal
   b. illegal
   c. mislegal
   d.translegal

13. A _____________ goes at the beginning of a root word.

a. defix
b. refix
c.misfix
d. prefix

14. Okay, class, let's _____________ what we've learned so far.

a. misview
b. deview
c. review
d. unview

15. If you _____________ cold pizza, it tastes pretty good.

a. reheat
b. misheat
c. unheat
d. deheat

Suffixes

Suffixes are like prefixes, except they go on the end of root words. Just like a prefix, a suffix changes the meaning of the root word. With a suffix, *teach* can become *teacher*. *Kind* can become *kindness*. *Friend* can become *friendly*. *Hope* can turn into *hopeless*, or it can turn into *hopeful*. *Tall* can turn into *taller*. We use many different suffixes every day. Let's practice with them.

For each problem, fill in the blank with the correct answer.

1. I'm sorry to hear about your accident, but I'm very ____________ you weren't hurt.
   a. thankness
   b. thankly
   c. thanker
   d. thankful

2. There aren't many choices, so you can't be too ____________.
   a. picky
   b. pickest
   c. pickful
   d. pickness

3. Her ____________ under stress helped everyone else relax.
   a. calmitude
   b. calmless
   c. calmness
   b. calmy

4. Bill throws a ____________ fastball.
   a. powery
   b. powerly
   c. powerful
   d. powerness

5. We're running late, so we have to move ____________.
 a. quickful
 b. quickly
 c. quicky
 d. quickless

6. Your cousin from England has a ____________ way of talking.
 a. delighter
 b. delightness
 c. delightly
 d. delightful

7. I was so ____________ that I went to bed early.
 a. sleepy
 b. sleepness
 c. sleeper
 d. sleeply

8. If we want to win, we have to practice ____________ than ever.
 a. hardful
 b. hardless
 c. harder
 d. hardly

9. He doesn't say much, but he's a very ____________ person.
 a. thoughtly
 b. thoughtful
 c.thoughtness
 d. thoughty

10. Your painting portrays your dog's face very ____________.
 a. niceful
 b. niceness
 c. niceless
 d. nicely

Understanding Latin Suffixes

Many of the words we use in English can be traced back to the language called Latin. Many of the suffixes we use to change the meanings of root words also come from Latin. Here are the most common Latin suffixes:

-able, -ible as in *breakable* or *edible*
-ty, -ity as in *loyalty* or *authority*
-ation as in *location* or *donation*
-fy, -ify as in *notify* or *horrify*
-ment as in *statement* or *pavement*

Draw a line from the word on the right that goes with the definition on the left

1. kings, queens, princes and princesses	celebration
2. money given to someone for doing something	terrify
3. scare the daylights out of	bendable
4. having nothing to eat for a long time	royalty
5. lights and appliances are powered by this	divisible
6 a big party	electricity
7 able to be bent	admirable
8 swear to tell the truth	testify
9 worthy of being looked up to	payment
10 able to be divided	starvation

Multisyllable Words

Put a slash (/) between syllables in each word below.
Here's an example: au/to/mat/ic

1. bowling
2. playground
3. basketball
4. soccer
5. referee
6. gymnast
7.goalpost
8. catcher
9. outfielder
10. baseball
11. quarterback
12. overtime
13. volleyball
14. tumbling
15. winner
16. tackle
17. scoreboard
18. fumble
19. strikeout
20. homer

Spelling Irregular Words

Most of the words we use every day in talking and writing follow regular patterns for spelling, and once you know the patterns, you can figure out how to spell a new word you've just heard. However, not all English words follow these patterns. These words are known as irregular words, and it's good to know them, because they come up a lot. Use the following exercise to improve your spelling of regular words.

Each sentence below has a blank space for a common word. Fill in the blank with the correct spelling from the four choices under each sentence.

1. Sally is my best ________.
   a. frend
   b. freind
   c. friend
   d. freand

2. My ________ baked us some cookies for a snack after lunch.
   a. moother
   b. muther
   c. mother
   d. muhther

3. Anyone who ________ like to try out can see me after class.
   a. wood
   b. wude
   c. would
   d. woold

4. My dad has quite a sense of ________.
   a. humor
   b. humur
   c. humer
   c. hughmer

5. There's a lot of work to do, so let's get ________.
   a. bussy
   b. bizy
   c. bizzy
   d. busy

6. State your ________ in feet and inches.
   a. hite
   b. heit
   c. heit
   d. height

7. You must watch your ________ to keep fit.
   a. weight
   b. wait
   c. wate
   d. whate

8. Go ________ to the principal's office, young man!
   a. strate
   b. straight
   c. strait
   d. streat

9. The book reports are due by next ________.
   a. Wenzday
   b. Wednesday
   c. Winsday
   d. Winsdy

10. They've _________ gone at least a week.
   a. ben
   b. been
   c. bin
   d. bean

11. What _________ of books do you like to read?
   a. kined
   b. kiend
   c. kind
   d. kynde

12. I need a _________ for my nose.
   a. tissue
   b. tishue
   c. tishoo
   d. tissioo

13. Some _________ are taller than men, but most aren't.
   a. wimmin
   b. wymmin
   c. whimmen
   d. women

14. Please pass the _________.
   a. shooger
   b. sugar
   c. shugerr
   d. shugor

15. I love funny movies because I like to _________.
   a. laff
   b. lagh
   c. lauff
   d. laugh

16. If it rains I _________ if we'll be able to finish the game.
  a. dout
  b. dought
  c. doute
  d. doubt

17. I _________ a comic book with my allowance.
  a. bot
  b. bought
  c. baught
  d. bout

18. My dad started his own _________ right after college.
  a. business
  b. bizness
  c. bisness
  d. bisuness

19. Well, Sammy, did you win or _________?
  a. loose
  b. luze
  c. louse
  d. lose

20. I'm so hungry I _________ eat a whole pizza!
  a. could
  b. cood
  c. coud
  d. cude

Writing

Opinion Essay

Choose one of the statements below. It can be a statement you agree with, or it can be one you don't agree with. Write a short essay saying how you feel about the statement.

Every family should have at least one pet.
Soccer is the best sport in the world.
Everyone should learn how to swim.
Watching too much TV is bad for you.
We should go to school all year long, instead of taking summer off.

After you choose one of the topics, write a few short paragraphs to express your feelings on the subject. You can agree or disagree; it doesn't matter. Start your essay by saying what statement you're talking about. Then say whether you agree or disagree with the statement. Next, give some reasons to explain why you feel the way you do about the topic. Then, using words like *therefore, since, because, for example*, show how your reasons connect to your opinion. Finally, write a few sentences to conclude and sum up everything. (You don't have to use all the space if you don't need it.)

Informational or Explanatory Essay

Choose a topic you know something about. Then write a brief essay talking about it, or explaining it. Pretend you're writing to someone that knows nothing about the topic, and you want to help them understand it. Start off by introducing the topic (saying what you're writing about), and give some background information about it. Then, talk about it in more detail, with examples, facts, details, etc. Use words like *and, another, also, more,* and *but* to connect ideas to each other. Then write a short conclusion. (You don't have to use all the space if you don't need it.)

Tell a Story

After you choose one of the topics, write a few short paragraphs to express your feelings on the subject. You can agree or disagree; it doesn't matter. Start your essay by saying what statement you're talking about. Then say whether you agree or disagree with the statement. Next, give some reasons to explain why you feel the way you do about the topic. Then, using words like *therefore, since, because, for example*, show how your reasons connect to your opinion. Finally, write a few sentences to conclude and sum up everything. (You don't have to use all the space if you don't need it.)

Conventions of Standard English

Parts of Speech

Do You Know the Parts of Speech?

Fill in the blanks with one of the words in the box.

Nouns	Adverbs	Adjectives	Verbs	Pronouns

1. ________ are words that tell us more about a person, place or thing.

2. ________ are words that represent people, places or things.

3. ________ are words that show action.

4. ________ are words that tell us more about an action.

5. ________ are words that take the place of nouns

Regular and Irregular Plural Nouns

Plural Nouns

With most nouns, it's easy to form a plural by simply adding -*s* to the end of the word. If a word end with a -*y*, change the -*y* to an -*I*, and add *es*. These are called regular nouns. Some nouns don't follow these rules, though. They are called irregular nouns. Let's look at some of them.

If a word ends in -*o*, add -*es*. So *potato* becomes *potatoes*.

If a word ends in -*f*, change the -*f* to -*v* and add -*es*. So *wolf* becomes *wolves*.

If a word ends in -*fe*, change the -*fe* to -*ve* and add *s*. So *knife* becomes *knives*.

Some words don't change, such as *sheep, shrimp* and *deer*. Other words don't really follow any of these rules. For instance, *person* becomes *people*.

Complete the following exercise using your knowledge of regular and irregular verbs. For each question, a singular noun is given. Write the plural form of the noun on the blank line beside it.

1. tornado ________

2. foot ________

3. fish ________

4. elf ________

5. tomato ________

6. man ________

7. calf ________

8. wife ________

9. town ________

10. mouse ________

Abstract Nouns

A noun is a word that names a person, place or thing. There are two kinds of nouns. Nouns in the first group are called *concrete nouns.* These words represent something you can see, hear, smell, touch or taste. Words like *cat, pudding, car, cloud, Tommy, mother, odor, cow, bank*, etc., are concrete nouns. However, some nouns represent things we can't see, hear, touch, taste, or smell. Words like *trust, sacrifice, honor, beauty, truth, obedience, thought, patience*, etc., are called *abstract nouns.*

In the sentences below, underline the abstract noun in each sentence.

1. I can't wait until Saturday!

2. Gina has a very pleasant attitude.

3. Micah, your duty will be to sweep the floor.

4. Our team won the championship!

5. I made an appointment with the doctor.

6. Mrs. Jones says I'm getting better at math.

7. Establish good habits and they will help you succeed.

8. Children, let's pledge allegiance to the flag.

9. Last year we had a lot of snow.

10. Hurry, because we don't have much time!

Concrete or Abstract?

In each sentence below, one word is underlined. If the word is an abstract noun, write A below the sentence. If the word is a concrete noun, write C below the sentence.

1. When is your <u>birthday</u>?

______

2. The <u>puppy</u> has a lot of energy.

______

3. Please pass the <u>salt</u>.

______

4. Having good <u>health</u> is better than having a lot of money.

______

5. I love reading about history.

____

6. I turned in my report to Mr. Alvarez.

____

7. It takes a lot of discipline to do well at school.

____

8. My cat had five kittens last night.

____

9. My house is three blocks away from the park.

____

10. We all need some help every now and then.

____

Regular and Irregular Verbs

With most verbs, changing from present tense to past tense is easy. All you do is add an *-ed* on the end, or duplicate the last letter of the word, and then add *-ed*. So *walk* becomes *walked*, and *hug* becomes *hugged*. Verbs like this are called regular verbs. Some verbs don't fit into this category, though. They are called irregular verbs.

Fun With Irregular Verbs

1. Buy me a hot dog while you're at the concession stand.

Yesterday I _________ a new comic book with my allowance.

2. Keep the noise down while I'm on the telephone, kids.

I _________ my sister's hamster in my room while she was at camp.

3. Hang the painting in the center of the wall.

After dinner, the family _________ ornaments on the Christmas tree.

4. I know a secret.

I _________ the secret before you did!

5. Class, meet me at the flagpole after the lunch bell rings.

After lunch, we _________ the teacher at the flagpole.

6. Put the groceries away, Tommy.

I _________ the groceries away an hour ago, Mom.

7. I go to Eastside Elementary.

I _________ to the science museum last Saturday.

8. If you want to lose weight, eat fewer snacks.

We _________ the game by one goal.

9. Bring me your homework, Melissa.

Last year, I _________ a turtle to class for show and tell.

10. Drink plenty of water on hot days.

Who _________ the last glass of milk?

Simple Verb Tenses

Verb Tenses

Verbs are words that show action. The action can be happening right now, or could be in the past, or in the future. We use different forms of verbs to show if a verb is past, present, or future. These forms are called tenses. So *I sing* is present tense, *I sang* is past tense, and *I will sing* is future tense.

What's Missing?

In each problem below, two verb tenses are shown, along with a blank line. Fill in the blank with the verb tense that is missing.

1. taste tasted ________

2. run will run ________

3. have had ________

4. kicked kick ________

5. will talk talked ________

6. will fly fly ________

7. sleep will sleep ________

8. spoke speak ________

9. woke will wake ________

10. will think think ________

Subject/Verb Agreement & Pronoun/Antecedent Agreement

Subject/Verb Agreement

A sentence is always about something. What the sentence is about is called the *subject* of the sentence. In many sentences, the subject is one person, place, or thing. In that case, the subject is singular. In sentences which are about more than one person, place or thing, the subject is plural. Singular subjects must have singular verbs, and plural subjects must have plural verbs. Singular verbs end in *-s* or *-es*. Plural verbs **don't** end in *-s* or *-es*.

meows	gallop
sings	hold
teach	reads
knows	ring
cuts	drink

1. Mrs. Jones and Ms. Sanchez both _________ 3rd grade at Eastside Elementary.

2. Santa _________ if you've been bad or good!

3. Our new cat _________ when he is hungry.

4. My big sister _________ in the choir at church.

5. I love to watch the horses _________ down the pasture.

6. Kids, _________ your juice and then we'll have dessert.

7. All the bells _________ at the same time.

8. Every year the teachers _________ a Halloween party for the entire school.

9. After lunch is over, every student _________ a book for 15 minutes.

10. Mr. Smith _________ his lawn at the same time every Saturday.

Match Those Subjects and Verbs!

In this passage, several verbs are in bold print. If the verb tense matches the subject, write R above the word (for Right). If the verb tense doesn't match the subject, write W above the word (for Wrong), and then write the correct word.

100,000 Miles a Year

Most people can't **imagine** driving over 100,000 miles in a year. That **are** a lot of driving! In fact, that would be enough miles to get a person almost halfway to the moon. Of course, you can't **drive** to the moon. You would have to fly in a rocket!

The average American **travels** only about 15,000 miles a year in a car. **Think** about your mother and father. If you're like most kids, your parents drive to jobs every day, and they also drive you to school activities. They also **takes** a few other short trips every week.

So who is driving over 100,000 miles a year? Professional truck drivers, that's who. They **goes** between 2000 and 2500 miles every week. It's a good thing they **does**, too. America **depend** on truck drivers. Truck drivers are the heartbeat of our nation's store delivery system. Almost everything people buy at a store was brought there by a truck driver. Truck drivers **makes** our lives much easier and more enjoyable.

Pronouns and Antecedents

Pretend a friend told you this:

Annette showed me Annette's new bicycle.

That would be very awkward, and it would sound silly. We don't keep repeating the name of a person, place or thing over and over. We use words called pronouns to take their place to avoid sounding awkward. This is how your friend would really tell you about the new bicycle:

Annette showed me her new bicycle.

There are lots of different pronouns. Words like *I, me, we, you, she, him, it, they, them, yours, mine, ours, his, hers,* and *theirs* are all pronouns. Some are singular, and some are plural. Which pronoun to use depends on the word the pronoun is replacing, or referring back to. That word is called the *antecedent*, which means something that comes before something else. In the sentence above, *Annette* is the antecedent, so the sentence needs a singular pronoun. A singular antecedent needs a singular pronoun, and a plural antecedent needs a plural pronoun. Also, some pronouns are personal pronouns, while others are pronouns that show possession. Words like *I, me, we, you, she, him, he, her, it, they,* and *them* are personal pronouns. Words like *my, mine, yours, his, hers, ours, theirs,* and *its* are possessive pronouns.

Keep Those Pronouns Straight!

After each sentence, circle the correct pronoun to fill in the blank.

1. I ate _______ lunch quickly so we could play outside.
my our mine its

2. The band members played _______ instruments perfectly.
yours their its theirs

3. Cindy shared ______ books with her friends.

theirs she they her

4. The cats like sitting in ______ lap.

theirs my its ours

5. If we don't hurry, the game will start without ______ .

he she us we

6. Omar has a red backpack, but ______ is blue.

mine my your their

7. Karen got up in front of the class and gave ______ book report.

theirs ours she her

8. Javier said ______ parents grew up in Peru.

him his its theirs

9. The team won ______ last three games.

its mine theirs us

10. Mom told my friends ______ were welcome to stay for supper.

they he she our

Pick That Pronoun!

Match the pronoun on the right by drawing a line to the word or phrase on the left it best fits.

Gabrielle	ours
belongs to him	it
Uncle Bob and Aunt Sally	us
Fred	she
belongs to you and me	theirs
belongs to me	he
you and me	my
belongs to the team	hers
belongs to her	they
the toy	his

Comparative and Superlative Adjectives and Adverbs

Adjectives: Comparative and Superlative

Adjectives describe nouns and pronouns. They tell us what kind of person, place or thing something is, like this:

Randy is tall.

The word *tall* tells us something about Randy. Some adjectives can help us compare or contrast different people, places, or things. These are called comparative adjectives and superlative adjectives. Here is a comparative adjective:

Randy is taller than his sister.

The word *taller* tells us something about two different people - Randy and his sister. We use comparative adjectives when discussing two people, places, or things. For comparing more than two, we use superlative adjectives, like this:

Randy is the tallest student in 3rd grade.

When you use comparative and superlative adjectives, there are some easy rules to follow.

For one syllable words, add *-er* to the end for comparative; add *-est* to the end for superlative. (If the adjective ends with *-e*, just add *-r* or *-st*.)

harder   softer   nicer   kindest   loudest

If the adjective is only one syllable and the last two letters are a short vowel followed by a consonant, duplicate the consonant and add *-er* or *-est*.

bigger   fattest   hotter

If the word ends in *-y*, change the *-y* to *-i*, and add *-er* for the comparative, or *-est* for the superlative.

sleepier   fuzzier   hungrier   silliest   happiest

For words that have more than one syllable, but don't end in *-y*, use the word *more* in front of it for the comparative; use the words *the most* in front of it for the superlative.

the most wonderful   more generous   more important   the most difficult   more interesting

If the adjective is only one syllable and the last two letters are a short vowel followed by a consonant, duplicate the consonant and add *-er* or *-est*.

bigger   fattest   hotter

There are a few adjectives that don't follow these rules. You probably know these already, because you use them all the time. Here are the two most common ones, along with their comparative and superlative forms:

good | better | best

bad | worse | worst

Pick the Right Adjective

An adjective is listed before each sentence. In each sentence, fill in the blank with the correct form of the adjective, either comparative or superlative. (Answers can be one or two words.)

1. MESSY
My desk is messy, but my closet is even ________.

2. FRIENDLY
Heather is the ________ girl I know.

3. TALL
Steve is tall, his sister is taller, and his older brother is the ________ .

4. BAD
This is the ________ thunderstorm I've ever seen.

5. HEAVY
This rock is _________ than that one.

6. ATHLETIC
I like sports a little, but my brother is _________ than I am.

7. SAD
That was the _________ story I've ever read.

8. LONG
Which is _________ , a yard or a meter?

9. ROUGH
Boy, this dirt road is the _________ one we've been on so far.

10. BIG
My baby brother is getting _________ every day.

Adverbs: Comparative and Superlative

Adverbs describe verbs; they tell us how, when, why or where the action took place. Some adverbs don't compare the word to anything else; these are called positive adverbs. Others compare between two actions; these are called comparative adverbs. If an adverb compares three or more actions, it is called a superlative adverb. Here's an example of all three:

Juan ran fast.

Billy ran faster than Juan.

Of the three runners, Cindy was the fastest.

Like many other parts of speech, most comparative and superlative adverbs follow a few basic rules.

In many cases, adverbs end in *-ly*. In these cases, simply put *more* in front of the word for the comparative form, or put *most* in front of the word for the superlative form.

For adverbs that don't end in *-ly*, simply add *-er* or *-est* to the end. There are a few irregular adverbs that don't follow either of these rules. Here are the main ones, in their positive, comparative and superlative forms.

well better best

badly worse worst

Fill in the Adverb

In front of each sentence is an adverb. Fill in the blank in each sentence using the correct form of the adverb. Answers can be one or two words.

1. QUICKLY Out of all the students, Joanna came up with the answer _________ .

2. LOUDLY One cow mooed _________ than the other cow.

3. WELL We played well, but unfortunately the other team played ________ .

4. PROMPTLY Class, this assignment needs to be completed ________ than last week's.

5. HARD I worked ______ than my brother and got done faster.

6. SLOW Grandpa usually drives _________ than Dad does.

7. RAPIDLY All the horses were fast, but Silver Flash galloped the ________ .

8. EARLY On Saturdays, I always wake up _________ than my sister.

9. SOON All three buses left together, but our bus arrived the _________ of all.

10. NEATLY Please organize your room _________ than you did the last time.

Coordinating and Subordinating Conjunctions

Simple, Compound and Complex Sentences

When it comes to sentence structures, there are three different kinds: simple, compound, and complex. Read this sentence:

I think horses are beautiful.

That's a **simple sentence**. It's called that because it expresses only one idea. That idea is an *independent clause*. It's independent because the idea makes sense all by itself; it's a complete thought.

Here's another sentence:

I think horses are beautiful, and I love to go horseback riding.

That is a **compound sentence**. That means it expresses two ideas, and both of them are independent clauses. To make it easier, just think of this sentence as two simple sentences joined together:

I think horses are beautiful. *I love to go horseback riding.*

A compound sentence always contains a word that joins the two independent clauses together. These words are called coordinating conjunctions. There are only seven coordinating conjunctions: *for, and, nor, but, or, yet, so*. An easy way to remember these is the make-believe word **FANBOYS**; each letter in FANBOYS is the first letter of one of the coordinating conjunctions.

Now look at this sentence:

I think horses are beautiful when they're galloping.

That's a **complex sentence**. It contains an independent clause, and a *dependent clause*. The words *they're galloping* make up a dependent clause - it depends on the rest of the sentence for its meaning. A complex sentence always contains a word or phrase that joins the independent clause to the dependent clause. These are called subordinating conjunctions, and there are many of them. Common ones include *while, after, wherever, where, whenever, unless, though, so that, since, now that, if, how, even though, even if, before, because, as soon as, as long as,* and *although*. The dependent clause can come before the independent clause, or it can come after.

Compound or Complex?

Read each sentence and decide if the sentence is a compound sentence, or a complex sentence. Write your answer in the blank space below the sentence.

1. Brian is going to the museum and Wendy is going to the bookstore.

____

2. Although he really didn't want to, Kent agreed to wear a tie to the restaurant.

____

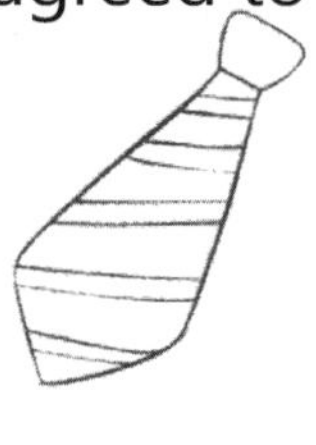

3. After we finish eating, we'll help Mom with the dishes.

____

4. I like pizza a lot, but I also like cheeseburgers.

____

5. If you do a little each day, you will never fall behind.

____

6. Since it's overcast, we had better take our umbrellas.

____

7. Whenever she's hungry, my cat rubs up against my ankles.

____

8. I got an A on my spelling test, and I got a B+ on my vocabulary test.

____

9. We can go to the park, or we can stay here and play.

____

10. Where there's a will, there's a way.

____

Make Your Own Compound Sentences

Each pair of sentences expresses two thoughts, followed by a coordinating conjunction. Rewrite them using one compound sentence, using the coordinating conjunction shown.

1. Fred has the flu. Carol has a cold. AND

____

2. I like baseball. I don't like basketball. BUT

____

3. You can eat lunch now. You can eat lunch later. OR

____

4. You should study hard. You can pass your test. SO

____

5. We read about art museums. Our teacher told us about famous painters. AND

____

Make Your Own Complex Sentences

Each pair of sentences expresses two thoughts, followed by a subordinating conjunction. Rewrite them using one complex sentence, using the subordinating conjunction shown.

1. The bell rings. It's time for lunch. WHEN

____

2. You're not feeling well. You should stay home. IF

____

3. You won't get dessert. You eat your vegetables. UNLESS

____

4. You must clean your room. You may go outside and play. BEFORE

____

5. Watch out for traffic. You ride your bike. WHILE

____

Capitalization in Titles

In titles of books, movies, etc, all words should be capitalized, except for the following (unless they are the first or last word in the title): *a, an, the, at, by, for, in, of, on, to, up, and, as, but, it, or, nor.*

Here are some examples:

Saved by the Bell

The Wind in the Willows

By the Light of the Silvery Moon

3. Fix Those Titles!

Here are ten titles. Follow the rules above to rewrite each one, using proper capitalization.

1. why you should exercise daily

____

2. now they tell me!

____

3. north to alaska

____

4. the hound of the baskervilles

____

5. a tale of two cities

____

6. please don't eat the daisies

____

7. indiana jones and the last crusade

____

8. uncle tom's cabin

____

9. the night before Christmas

____

10. willy wonka and the chocolate factory

Commas in Addresses

Commas and Quotation Marks in Dialogue

When you write a city and a state, or a city and a country, you need a comma between them.

Ukiah, California

London, England

Commas are also necessary in dialogue, (when people are talking), along with quotation marks. Look at these sentences:

"Hurry up," Mrs. Smith said, "or you'll be late for school."

Heather said, "That's a lovely hat, Grandmother."

Mrs. Gonzalez asked, "Students, are you ready for the big surprise?"

The commas and quotation marks help us understand what is being said, and help keep us from being confused. Quotation marks always come in pairs, too - one at the beginning of the dialogue being quoted, and one at the end. The last quotation mark should come after the period, question mark or exclamation point.

Commas and Quotations

In the following sentences or addresses, add commas, quotation marks, and other punctuation as needed.

1. Boise Idaho

____

2. Mom doesn't want us to have snacks before supper Billy reminded Joanie

____

3. Freida asked What time does the bus usually get here

____

4. Sir Pedro exclaimed you dropped your wallet

____

5. Paris France

____

6. Are those your sunglasses Molly asked

____

7. James and Kirk said Mr. Brown you need to see me after class

____

8. Des Moines Iowa

____

9. Dad said, Let's go to the beach this Saturday

____

10. I don't think that's a very good idea Mabel her mother replied.

____

Possessives

Possessives are words that show that something belongs to someone or something, or has a strong relationship with someone or something. Here are two examples.

That is Bob's bike.

She is Doris's mother.

If the word is a plural, simply add an apostrophe to the end of the word, like this:

The girls' teacher asked them to work on a project together.

The teams' coaches got into a big argument.

The words *my, mine, ours, his, hers, yours, its, their*, and *their*s are also possessives.

It's Raining Cats and Possessives!

Each sentence below sounds awkward. Rewrite each one using a possessive, as in the example shown.

This ball belongs to them.
*This is their ball.*__________

1. Let's say hello to the mom of Tanequa.

____

2. This is the uniform that belongs to Jack.

____

3. I rode the new bike that belongs to Freddy.

____

4. Here's the bib that belongs to the baby.

____

5. The stall that belongs to the horse needs cleaned.

____

6. Here's the book that belongs to you.

____

7. This is the new video game that belongs to Charles.

____

8. The bus that you ride is coming.

____

9. The dog wagged the tail that belongs to the dog.

____

10. The fingers of the boys were freezing after they built the snowman.

____

High Frequency Words | Base Words and Suffixes

Scrambled Words & Toast

Unscramble the mixed up word in each problem and write it in the blank below.

1. A talking fish? That's mispsiboel!

____

2. I'll have to ask my parents, but I bporably will be able to attend your birthday party.

____

3. Okay, vebreoydy, we need to keep the noise down.

____

4. I hope the awtehre is nice when we go camping.

____

5. Don't litter – help keep America aebutiufl.

____

6. All the dresses on sale look nice, but this one's the petirtets.

____

7. We all alehdug at the funny clown.

____

8. Students, don't yell. Raise your hand if you have a utesoqni.

____

9. We practiced every day ebaucse we wanted to win.

____

10. In what year did Columbus idcrsove America?

____

Base Words and Suffixes

We can add a suffix to many words to make a new word. Some of these suffixes are *-ion, -ment, -ing, -y, -al, -ive, -est, -ation, -ed, -ation, -able, -ly, -ful, -ment,* and *-less*. If the base word end in a silent *-e*, and the suffix begins with a vowel, drop the *-e*. This includes suffixes that start with *-y*.

Add a suffix to the base word listed in front of each sentence to make a new word to complete the sentence.

1. SCARE Boy, some of those stories around the campfire were really _________ .

2. EXCITE That was one of the most _________ basketball games I've ever seen.

3. INTEREST I'm sorry, but I just didn't find the book to be very _________ .

4. REPLACE Class, Ms. Brown is sick today, so I will be her _________ .

5. NEW These are the _______ versions; they just came out.

6. HOPE It's _________; we'll never dig a hole to China at this rate.

7. MUD My boots were really _________ after our hike in the rain.

8. ACCIDENT I didn't do it on purpose; it was _________ .

9. HAPPY Working in his garden brings Grandpa much _________ .

10. MUSIC There are nearly 50 _________ in the marching band.

Choose words and phrases for effect

There are many ways of talking or writing about similar things, using different words. Some words have almost the same meaning as other words, but leave a different impression on the listener or reader. You can choose what effect to have on the reader or listener by choosing which words to use. Let's practice.

What's the Good Word?

For each problem, there will be three choices. Circle the one that is the best choice.

1. If someone asked you how you felt about a test coming up in ten minutes, and you weren't ready at all, and you were pretty sure you were going to fail, what would be the best way to phrase it to make your feelings clear?
   a. I'm anxious.
   b. I'm nervous.
   c. I'm worried.

2. Which of these sentences is the most appropriate?
   a. In the middle of a daydream, Becky was startled by the classroom bell.
   b. In the middle of a daydream, Becky was shocked by the classroom bell.
   c. In the middle of a daydream, Becky was terrified by the classroom bell.

3. Which sentence best expresses the idea that a comedian was extremely funny?
   a. The comedian was humorous.
   b. The comedian was hilarious.
   c. The comedian was amusing.

4. Which of these sentences gives the right effect?
   a. I thought I would die chuckling.
   b. I thought I would die snickering.
   c. I thought I would die laughing.

5. How would a person who can hardly believe how tall and heavy an elephant is try to communicate its size to someone else?
   a. The elephant was large.
   b. The elephant was huge.
   c. The elephant was big.

6. If you loved to play in the snow, what would your reaction be if you woke up one day to find a foot of snow outside?
   a. This is nice.
   b. This is neat.
   c. This is wonderful.

7. If you saw a car go by your house at a high rate of speed, which of these sentences would be the best way to describe it?
   a. The car went past my house.
   b. The car streaked past my house.
   c. The car drove past my house.

8. Which of these sentences sounds nicest?
   a. Oh, what an obese little baby!
   b. Oh, what an overweight little baby!
   c. Oh, what a chubby little baby!

9. Which of these sentences sounds the least like boasting?
   a. We defeated the other team.
   b. We trounced the other team.
   c. We destroyed the other team.

10. Which sentence is the best for describing the story of Paul Bunyan and Babe?
   a. It is a tall tale
   b. It is a lie.
   c. It is a falsehood.

Differences between spoken and written English

The rules we follow when we talk are different than the rules we use when writing. Writing is considered to be formal, while talking is informal, or relaxed. Slang is fine when we're talking with friends, but is not acceptable in letters to people we don't know well. When we talk, we use lots of contractions, such as *don't, can't, didn't, shouldn't,* etc. When writing, these are frowned upon, except in writing dialogue, or penning a note or letter to a good friend. When we're talking, we can use our voice and our body language to communicate, as well as our words, so we don't need to be quite as exact in our phrasing. In writing, we can only use words and punctuation to get our message across, so we need to be more precise when choosing our words.

Spoken or Written?

Read each sentence, and decide if it's more appropriate as a spoken sentence, or a written sentence. Write S for spoken or W for written underneath the sentence.

1. Who was that dude I saw you talking to?

____

2. The weather forecast for Saturday does not sound promising for our picnic.

____

3. I would like to return the item I purchased and request a refund.

____

4. That'll teach 'em!

____

5. What's up?

____

6. Whatever you say, pal!

____

7. I want to express my strong disapproval of the ordinance which has been proposed.

____

8. Refreshments will be provided.

____

9. What's up with that?

____

10. We would like to invite you to come visit us at Christmas.

____

Determine meaning of new word when affix is added to known word

Use a known root word as a clue to the meaning of an unknown word with the same root

What Does It Mean?

Each sentence has one underlined word, which contains a prefix or a suffix. Use your knowledge of the root word to figure out the definition of the new word, and circle the correct answer.

1. Being near a loud siren can be very unpleasant.
   a. fun
   b. enjoyable
   c. not enjoyable

2. If you are overconfident you may fail the test.
   a. not confident enough
   b. having too much confidence
   c. a little confident

3. Charles Lindbergh made the first solo transatlantic flight.
   a. across the Atlantic Ocean
   b. into the Atlantic Ocean
   c. under the Atlantic Ocean

4. My little brother gets hyperactive when he eats too much sugar.
   a. not active
   b. less active
   c. very active

5. After his team won the game, Jack became <u>boastful</u>.
   a. not boasting very much
   b. not boasting at all
   c. boasting a lot

6. Teresa is the most <u>unfriendly</u> person I know.
   a. not friendly
   b. very friendly
   c. popular

7. Don't let one bad grade <u>discourage</u> you.
   a. give lots of courage
   b. take away courage
   c. give a little more courage

8. You acted <u>honorably</u>, Sandy.
   a. in an honorable way
   b. not in an honorable way
   c. in a confused way

9. We must <u>preheat</u> the oven for fifteen minutes.
   a. heat the oven after putting the food in
   b. heat the oven before putting the food in
   c. heat the oven while the food is in

10. The snowfall made for a <u>wondrous</u> sight the next morning.
   a. ugly
   b. boring
   c. full of wonder

Make a New Word

Using a suffix or prefix, fill in the blank with letters to change the word to match the definition shown.

1. not agree = ___agree
2. not believable = _believable
3. state of being happy = happ_____
4. do again = _do
5. not polite = _polite
6. in a quick manner = quick_
7. state of being aware = aware____
8. person who teaches = teach_
9. having a magic quality = magic_
10. possessing caution = cauti___

Practice Test #1

Practice Questions

Questions 1 - 11 pertain to the following passage:

Miguel's World

Old Logs Help Animals

1. Miguel Gonzalez and his father took many walks in the woods near their house. When Miguel was very young, around five, he liked to pick up branches and hit them against the ground and the trees. Sometimes he would waive the stick and pretend he was fighting a great battle. Mr. Gonzalez always told Miguel to drop the stick.

2. "You will poke an eye out," said Mr. Gonzalez. A few years later, Miguel stopped hitting with sticks and started asking his father about the trees and other things he saw in the woods. Miguel's father told him how to identify different trees by the texture of their bark and the size and shape of their leaves. Miguel found out how trees spread their seeds and what kinds of animals eat the leaves, bark, and seeds. Miguel loved taking walks with his father, but he did not appreciate all the things that he saw in the woods. One day they almost tripped over a log that had fallen on the trail. Miguel kicked it.

3. "Stupid log, it almost made me fall," he said. Miguel's father waved his arms, shook his head, and told his son to stop. "That's not just a piece of wood, Miguel," said Mr. Gonzalez. "That log is a home for many creatures and plants. Kicking that log would be like an earthquake to them! How would you like it

if a giant ant kicked our house?"
4. "There are ants in there?" asked Miguel.
"Watch," said Mr. Gonzalez. He brushed the old brown leaves and rotting bark off the top of the log until they could see the wood buried underneath. On the smooth surface were clusters of small dark holes. An ant poked its head from one of the holes. Miguel laughed.
5. "Is there anything else in that log?" Miguel asked.
"Let's see," said Mr. Gonzalez. The two brushed off more leaves. They worked carefully to avoid touching the slimy slugs that dotted the log. Near the end of the rotten piece of timber was a large rough hole. A squirrel darted out from the hole and chattered noisily. On the nearby trees, birds called and sang noisily, too.

6. "They're waiting for us to leave so they can eat," smiled Mr. Gonzalez. "Those ants and slugs may not seem tasty to us, but they are a gourmet treat for the birds."
"Let's go," said Miguel. "They look hungry, and I hate making them wait for lunch."
7. After a few minutes, Miguel turned suddenly and started walking quickly in the opposite direction, back toward the log.
"Hey, what are you doing? What's up?" called Miguel's father.
Miguel stopped and turned around. "We left the log uncovered. If we don't put the leaves and bark back where we found them, the ants won't have anywhere to hide."
8. Miguel's father laughed and started to jog toward his son. "A little while ago you hated that log. Now you want to protect it."
"You always told me, treat others as you want to be treated," said Miguel with a smile. "I'm just following your advice!"

1. Paragraph 1 is mostly about:

Ⓐ The woods near Miguel's house

Ⓑ Miguel's father's love for nature

Ⓒ Miguel's behavior during walks

Ⓓ How sticks can be used as weapons

2. How did Miguel change when he got older?

Ⓐ He became more frightened of the woods

Ⓑ He became more dangerous toward his father

Ⓒ He became more bored with his father

Ⓓ He became more interested in the woods

3. Which meaning best fits the way the word "identify" is used in paragraph 2?

Ⓐ To become the same

Ⓑ To understand well

Ⓒ To recognize

Ⓓ To symbolize

4. Where does this story take place?

Ⓐ In a forest

Ⓑ In a park

Ⓒ In a garden

Ⓓ In an orchard

5. Which of the following words best describes Miguel's reaction when he learns that ants live in logs?

Ⓐ Happy

Ⓑ Confused

Ⓒ Angry

Ⓓ Sad

6. What is the title of this article?

Ⓐ Miguel Gonzalez

Ⓑ Miguel's World

Ⓒ Old Logs Help Animals

Ⓓ By Martha Gold

7. Why were the birds in paragraph 5 making so much noise?

Ⓐ Miguel had messed up their nest

Ⓑ Miguel kicked the log

Ⓒ They wanted to eat the bugs that Miguel had uncovered in the log

Ⓓ The squirrel was making noise and they wanted to be louder

8. Read the chart below. It shows the order in which some events happened in the story.

Miguel played with sticks during walks in the woods with his father.
⇩
⇩
Miguel and his father walk away so the birds can eat the ants and slugs in the log.
⇩
Miguel runs back to the log to put the leaves and bark back on top of the log.

Which of the following statements belongs in the empty box?

Ⓐ Miguel's father tells him not to kick the log.

Ⓑ Miguel laughs at the ants.

Ⓒ Miguel gets angry and goes home.

Ⓓ Miguel's father sits on the log.

9. Which sentence from the story showed that Miguel changed his mind?

Ⓐ "You always told me, treat others as you want to be treated"

Ⓑ "A little while ago you hated that log. Now you want to protect it."

Ⓒ "They look hungry, and I hate making them wait for lunch."

Ⓓ "If we don't put the leaves and bark back where we found them, the ants won't have anywhere to hide."

10. What will Miguel probably do from now on if he comes across a log in the trail?

Ⓐ He will push the log out of the way

Ⓑ He will kick the log out of the way

Ⓒ He will turn back and walk home

Ⓓ He will look for animals in the log

11. What does this picture from the story most likely represent?

Ⓐ Miguel's father tells him not to kick the log

Ⓑ Miguel asking his father a question as they walk through the woods

Ⓒ Miguel playing with a stick in the woods

Ⓓ Miguel's father tripping over the log

Questions 12 - 17 pertain to the following passage:

My name is Tanya, and I have a dog whose name is Maize. I found her one summer in the parking lot of a supermarket when she was a puppy. I was taking our cart back to the store when I saw a small black and white animal dart under a row of shopping carts next to the main door. It moved so fast, all I saw was a blur. I did not know if the animal was a cat, a dog, or a skunk until it started barking.

My mom always told me not to play with strange animals, but something about Maize seemed safe. I bent down to find her under the carts and called to her. She came creeping out, slowly at first. Then she ran straight to me, wagging her tail. I picked her up and brought her back to my mom.
"Look what I found!" I said, holding up Maize, as she licked my face.
"No," said my mom.

I was about to protest when the puppy leaned over to my mom and licked her hand. Then she tried to lick my mom's face. My mom started to laugh.

"You are cute!" she said to the puppy. "It's hard to say no to a kiss like that."

"Can we keep her?" I asked.

"If you take care of her," said Mom. "You have to feed her, take her out for walks, and train her to behave."

At first, I was excited to have a dog. Maize slept on my bed and woke me up every morning by jumping on my bed. I took her for long walks in the park. Then school started, and I had to wake up early to take Maize outside before I got on the bus. I had to fill her food and water bowls as soon as I got home. I could not go to my friends' houses because I had to be home to take care of Maize. I started to wish I had not found Maize.

One Friday afternoon I was walking down my street when I saw my best friend, Laticia.

"Hey Tanya!" Laticia called. "Is that Maize?"

"Yes," I said.

"Wait here," said Laticia. "I am going to ask my mom if I can come over to play with you guys."

After a few minutes, Laticia came back. "Mom said I can come over for an hour, so let's go," she said.

We had a great time—Laticia, Maize, and me. Now my friends come over to my house to play all the time. They want to see me and play with Maize. I'm so glad I found Maize. She's the best friend a girl could have.

This question has two parts. Answer Part A, then answer Part B.

12. Part A: Which words help the reader understand the meaning of the word "dart" in the first paragraph?

Ⓐ Until it started barking

Ⓑ It moved so fast

Ⓒ A small black and white animal

Ⓓ Under a row

Part B: Based on your answer in Part A, what do you think "dart" means?

Ⓐ a sharp pointed object

Ⓑ an animal

Ⓒ a quick movement

Ⓓ to hide under something

13. Why did Tanya think Maize was a skunk?

Ⓐ Skunks live under shopping carts.

Ⓑ Dogs are not black and white.

Ⓒ Skunks are black and white.

Ⓓ Tanya smelled something bad.

14. What is the main problem in the story?

Ⓐ Tanya's mom won't let her keep Maize

Ⓑ Tanya's friends don't like Maize

Ⓒ Maize is messing up the house during the day

Ⓓ Tanya can't visit her friends after school

15. How did Laticia solve Tanya's problem?

Ⓐ Laticia went over to Tanya's house

Ⓑ Tanya went to Laticia's house

Ⓒ Tanya gave Maize away

Ⓓ Tanya and her mom went to the supermarket

16. What title would be the best choice for this story?

Ⓐ Tanya's New Best Friend

Ⓑ Maize is Crazy

Ⓒ Dogs are Difficult

Ⓓ Laticia Comes Over

17. According to the story, what all is required to take care of a dog? Select all that apply.

I. Feed them
II. Groom them
III. Take them for walks
IV. Take them on trips
V. Train them to behave

Questions 18 - 24 pertain to the following passage:

The Animal Times

<u>Bats Our Flying Friends by Martha Gold</u>

Most people are afraid of bats. They are scared of their sharp teeth. They are scared because bats only come out at night. People worry that bats will bite them, but bats do not feed on people. Most bats in North America eat insects that they catch in the air with their teeth. Some bats eat mice, birds, frogs, lizards, and other bats. One kind of bat in Mexico catches fish in the claws of its hind legs. In Asia, large bats called Flying Foxes eat fruit. Other bats with long noses drink sweet juice from flowers.

All bats are mammals. They are the only mammals that fly. Bats live everywhere in the world except Antarctica and the North Pole. Most bats do not drink blood. Only vampire bats drink blood. Vampire bats live in Central and South America. They land on animals and bite them to make a tiny cut. Then they lap up the blood with their tongues. Vampire bats rarely bite people. If they do bite, they do not take much blood. However, bats may carry germs that cause disease.

Bats are not good pets, but they are useful to people. They eat insects, mice and other pests. Some cultures even think bats bring good luck!

18. Which of the following choices names the foods that bats eat?

Ⓐ fox, pets, cats, dogs

Ⓑ mice, blood, fish, insects

Ⓒ noses, teeth, claws, legs

Ⓓ flowers, seeds, nuts, grass

19. Where do bats NOT live?

Ⓐ Central and South America

Ⓑ Antarctica

Ⓒ Asia

Ⓓ North America

20. Which of the following are ways that bats are helpful to people? Select all that apply.

I. They eat insects
II. They carry diseases
III. They eat fruit
IV. They eat mice and other pests
V. They only come out at night

21. Fill in the blank in the following sentence. Bats are the only mammals that ___________.

Ⓐ have teeth

Ⓑ eat bugs

Ⓒ eat fruit

Ⓓ fly

22. Look at the diagram below about flying foxes and vampire bats, and then answer the question that follows.

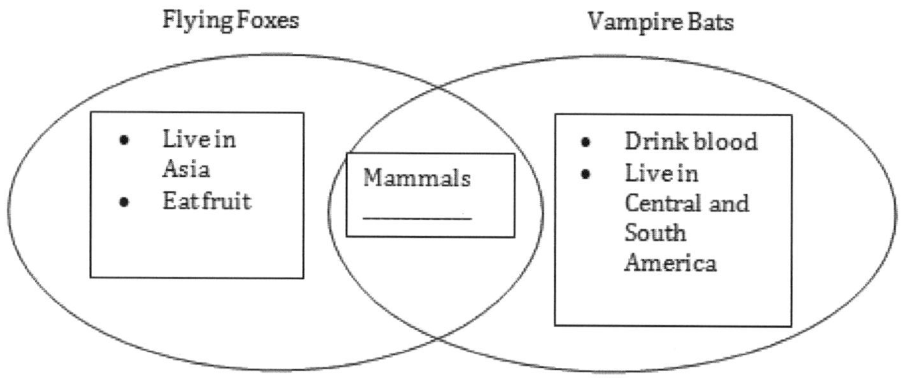

Which of the following belongs in the blank?

Ⓐ Bite animals and sometimes people

Ⓑ Eat insects

Ⓒ Make good pets

Ⓓ Only come out at night

23. What is the title of this article?

Ⓐ Bats: Our Flying Friends

Ⓑ Animal Times by Martha Gold

Ⓒ Animal Times

Ⓓ By Martha Gold

24. Which of the following is a trait that most bats in North America have?

Ⓐ Bite animals and sometimes people

Ⓑ Come out in the daytime

Ⓒ Eat insects

Ⓓ Catch fish with its claws

Questions 25 -31 pertain to the following passage:

<u>Sam, My Teddy Bear</u>

When I was just a child of three, I got a teddy bear.
With a squeeze, I called him Sam, and I took him everywhere,
to my grandma's, the babysitter's, the doctor's and the pool.
Sometimes big kids would laugh at me, but my friends thought
Sam was cool.
But all that travel took its toll on Sam's good looks.
His fur wore off in patches and his ears bent into crooks.
Now he stays put on a shelf,
next to some blocks and a small green elf.
I still love Sam and would never give him away,
but I'm too old for teddy bears, so in my room he'll stay.

25. What choice best summarizes this poem?

Ⓐ Sam wore out after a few years. His fur was in patches and his ears were bent. He looked old

Ⓑ A girl got a teddy bear for a present and took it everywhere. Then she got bored with it

Ⓒ A girl got a teddy bear for a present and loved it. After taking it everywhere with her, she outgrew it, but she still loves it

Ⓓ The girl took the bear everywhere, to her grandmother's, the babysitter's and the pool. Kids laughed at her

26. How old was the author when she got the bear?

Ⓐ Three

Ⓑ Two

Ⓒ Four

Ⓓ Five

27. What did the author do when she first got the bear?

Ⓐ Laughed at him

Ⓑ Took him everywhere

Ⓒ Put him on a shelf

Ⓓ Gave him away

28. What choice shows how Sam looked after a few years?

Ⓐ "My friends thought Sam was cool"

Ⓑ "His fur wore off in patches"

Ⓒ "Sometimes big kids would laugh at me"

Ⓓ "Next to some blocks and a small, green elf"

29. What choice shows the author no longer takes Sam everywhere?

Ⓐ "All that travel had its toll on Sam's good looks"

Ⓑ "Next to some blocks and a small green elf"

Ⓒ "I still love Sam and would never give him away"

Ⓓ "But I'm too old for teddy bears, so in my room he'll stay"

This question has two parts. Answer Part A, then answer Part B.

30. Part A: In this poem, where are the rhyming words?

Ⓐ at the end of every other line

Ⓑ at the end of every very third line

Ⓒ at the end of every two lines

Ⓓ at the end of every three lines

Part B: Which word rhymes with "looks"?

Ⓐ pool

Ⓑ cool

Ⓒ crooks

Ⓓ good

31. What is the correct order of events in this poem?

Ⓐ Child receives Sam. Child takes Sam everywhere. Child puts Sam on a shelf

Ⓑ Child puts Sam on a shelf. Child takes Sam everywhere. Child receives Sam

Ⓒ Child takes Sam everywhere. Child receives Sam. Child puts Sam on a shelf

Ⓓ Child receives Sam. Child puts Sam on a shelf. Child takes Sam everywhere

Questions 32 - 40 pertain to the following passage:

<u>Fire Needs Fuel and More to Burn</u>

On the ground lay a dead tree, its branches sticking out like a porcupine's quills. Jake started breaking off the branches and putting them in a pile. His father had sent him to find kindling wood for their fire.

"What's kindling wood?" Jake asked.

"Boy! You've been living in the city too long, Jake!" said Jake's father. "Kindling is little branches no thicker around than this." He held up his hand and made a circle with his first finger and thumb. "We need them to start the fire."

Jake measured the circumference of the branches by wrapping his first finger and thumb around each one. If the thumb and finger touched, he put it in the pile. If his finger and thumb could not touch, he left it on the tree. After he had collected an armful, Jake brought the pile of branches to his father.

His father was crumpling newspaper and arranging it around the cement circle that held up an iron grill. The wood was dry, brown, and old, but not rotten.

"Perfect kindling, Jake," said his father. "Good job!"

He piled the kindling on top of the newspapers and lit a match. The flames crept up the corners and edges of the paper and curled around the sticks. Soon the flames were flickering, and Jake's father put on the first log.

"What makes fire burn?" asked Jake, as he set out plates and cups on the picnic table for dinner.
"Three things," said his father. "I'll give you a hint. You are breathing one of them right now."

"Smoke?" asked Jake, coughing.

"Oxygen," said Jake's father, laughing. "The wood we're using is another. Wood is fuel, paper is fuel, and gasoline is fuel. Anything that can burn is fuel. Finally, you need high heat, called the kindling temperature, so the fuel will catch fire and make flames."
"How hot does the kindling temperature have to be?" asked Jake.

"It's different for different kinds of fuel," said Jake's father. "For wood it is about 500°F (260°C). Some fuels need a higher kindling temperature, and some need a lower temperature."

Jake looked down at the fire. The flames crept around the log and started to catch on to the bark. The flames flickered around the iron bars, but the bars did not burn.

"Why doesn't the iron in the grill burn?" asked Jake.

"It's fireproof," said Jake's father. "Oxygen cannot mix with it, so it cannot burn. It is the same with stone or brick."

"It's a good thing," said Jake, as he unwrapped the hotdogs. "Or we would have to order out for pizza!"

32. Where are Jake and his father?

Ⓐ In a cabin

Ⓑ At a campsite

Ⓒ At a lake

Ⓓ Next to a river

33. In the second paragraph, what does the word "circumference" mean?

Ⓐ The distance around a circle

Ⓑ The distance across a circle

Ⓒ The distance across a stick

Ⓓ The distance along a stick

34. There were four good things about the kindling that Jake brought back. List three of them.

____

____

____

35. What is the right combination to make fire?

Ⓐ Fuel + food + air

Ⓑ Fuel + kindling heat + wood

Ⓒ Fuel + oxygen + food

Ⓓ Fuel + oxygen + kindling heat

36. What is the order of events in this story?

Ⓐ Jake takes out hotdogs. Jake gets kindling wood. Jake's father starts the fire

Ⓑ Jake's father starts the fire. Jake takes out hotdogs. Jake gets kindling wood

Ⓒ Jake's father starts the fire. Jake gets kindling wood. Jake takes out hotdogs

Ⓓ Jake gets kindling wood. Jake's father starts the fire. Jake takes out hotdogs

37. How hot is the kindling temperature for wood?

Ⓐ 600°F

Ⓑ 260°F

Ⓒ 500°F

Ⓓ 700°F

38. What does the small round circle after the temperature mean?

Ⓐ Hot

Ⓑ Temperature

Ⓒ Degrees

Ⓓ Cold

39. Why would Jake and his father have had to order pizza if iron burned?

Ⓐ Because the grill would have burned up

Ⓑ Because the hotdogs would not have tasted good

Ⓒ Because the fire would have gone out

Ⓓ Because the kindling temperature of iron is 500°F

40. The next time Jake goes camping, what will he bring to start a fire?

Ⓐ Matches, food, grill

Ⓑ Matches, grill, paper

Ⓒ Matches, hotdogs, paper

Ⓓ Wood, fuel, paper

Practice Test #2

Practice Questions

Questions 1 - 9 pertain to the following passage:

Snacks Made Easy By Martha Gold

After school, Mika came running from the school bus into her house.

Mom, I'm starving," she said, dropping her school bag on the kitchen floor and opening the refrigerator. "What do we have to eat?"

"Not much," said her mother. "I have to go shopping today."

"Do we still have those cheese crackers?" asked Mika.

"We're all out," said Mika's mother. "If you want, we can make some."

"MAKE them?" asked Mika. "You mean with cheese and stuff?"

"There is a recipe I want to try," said Mika's mother. "Why don't we make some? Then we can go shopping."

"But I want something NOW," whined Mika.

"Have some fruit," said her mother, holding out an apple.

"Okay," said Mika, taking the apple. "Now, how do you make these crackers?"

Mika's mother put a sheet of paper on the kitchen table in front of her. On the paper was a recipe, or directions, on how to make cheese crackers.

<u>Cheese Crackers</u>

Ingredients:

1-cup all-purpose flour and a little

Extra flour to roll out dough
1/2-teaspoon salt
4 tablespoons cold butter
8 ounces grated cheese
(Cheddar or Monterey Jack)
1/4-cup of water

Cooking Utensils:
1 large mixing bowl
1 measuring cup
1/2-teaspoon measure
Mixing spoon
Rolling pin
Cookie cutters
2 table knives or potato masher

Directions:

1. Heat the oven to 350° F.
2. Cut the butter into small pieces.
3. Mix the flour and salt together in a large bowl.
4. Add the butter and cut it into the flour using two table knives or a potato masher. Cut until the pieces of butter are smaller than a pea.
5. Add the water gradually, one tablespoon at a time. Mix it in until the dough sticks together in a ball.
6. Cover the bowl with plastic wrap. Put it in the refrigerator for half-an-hour.
7. Sprinkle flour on a clean table or on the counter. Put the dough in the middle of the flour.
8. Roll out the dough until it is as thick as a regular-sized magazine. Cut out shapes using small cookie cutters.
   9. Place the shapes on a greased, non-stick cookie sheet. Bake for 15 minutes, or until the crackers are golden brown. Let cool and enjoy!

1. What is the title of this story?

Ⓐ Snacks Made Easy

Ⓑ Cheese Crackers

Ⓒ By Martha Gold

Ⓓ Snacks Made Easy By Martha Gold

2. Which two cheeses does the recipe recommend using? Fill in the blanks with your answer.

____

____

3. What did Mika mean when she said, "But I want something NOW," after her mother asked to make crackers?

Ⓐ Mika did not want cheese crackers

Ⓑ Mika wanted an apple

Ⓒ Mika wanted to go shopping

Ⓓ Mika was hungry

4. What does the word "ingredient" mean?

Ⓐ A statement that tells how to do something

Ⓑ One of the items used to make a food.

Ⓒ The temperature at which the food should bake

Ⓓ A name for the recipe

This question has two parts. Answer Part A, then answer Part B.

5. Part A: What ingredient would you need in order to complete step 2?

Ⓐ Flour

Ⓑ Butter

Ⓒ Salt

Ⓓ Pepper

Part B: What other step is this ingredient used in?

Ⓐ Step 3

Ⓑ Step 4

Ⓒ Step 5

Ⓓ Step 6

6. Which of the following meanings best fits the way "gradually" is used in step 5?

Ⓐ A little at a time

Ⓑ Slowly

Ⓒ Not steep

Ⓓ Continuously

7. Why did the author number the steps in the directions?

Ⓐ Because letters were too confusing

Ⓑ To know how long the recipe takes to make

Ⓒ To show that it is important to complete the steps in order

Ⓓ For cooks who prefer to read numbers

8. Which answer should go in the blank?

What happens	*Why it happens*
Mika reads the cheese crackers recipe.	___________________________

Ⓐ Mika wants to make cheese crackers

Ⓑ Mika wants to go shopping

Ⓒ Mika wants another apple

Ⓓ Mika wants a different snack

9. What will Mika probably do in the future when she wants cheese crackers?

Ⓐ Open the refrigerator and look for them

Ⓑ Ask her mother to buy some at the store

Ⓒ Ask her mother to help her make some

Ⓓ Eat an apple instead

Questions 10 - 18 pertain to the following passage:

An Unforgettable Day at the History Museum by Martha Gold

1. Hakeem's third-grade class takes a field trip every spring to the county historical museum. The county historian gives the class a tour and afterward sets the students loose to explore the museum. Hakeem's older brother, Gerard, went two years earlier. Gerard said the museum was great except for one room.

"Watch out for the room with the old war uniforms, it's haunted," said Gerard at dinner one night.

"What do you mean, haunted?" asked Hakeem.

2. "We heard funny noises in the room," said Gerard. "We

looked around to see if anyone else was there, but it was empty. Then Sammy swore he saw the eyes of one of the costume dummies move around, as if it were watching us. We were so scared we left before we got to the end of the exhibit."

"Gerard, stop scaring your brother," said Hakeem's mother. "Hakeem, there is no such thing as ghosts. I'm sure there is a logical explanation for those noises. As for the eyes moving, that's just Sammy's imagination getting out of hand."

3. Stories about ghosts usually do not frighten Hakeem. He laughed at all the ghost stories his counselor told at camp last summer around the campfire. He watched scary movies with his babysitter and felt fine. But something about Gerard's words made Hakeem feel uneasy. Gerard does not usually joke around. Hakeem doubted that Gerard was just trying to scare him. Instead, Gerard was probably trying to warn him.

4. On the day of the field trip, Hakeem asked his teacher, Mr. Orwell, about Gerard's story as they rode the bus to the museum.

"It's an old building," said Mr. Orwell. "The floor boards creak and I'm sure there are other parts of the museum that make strange noises. It's not haunted, just a little creepy."
"What about the eyes watching Sammy?" asked Hakeem.

Mr. Orwell laughed. "Sammy's got a great imagination," he said. "I'm sure that's what made him think the statue was watching him."

5. After the tour, Hakeem walked around the museum with his best friend Malcolm. Malcolm wanted to see the old war uniforms, but Hakeem was nervous. Finally, he agreed to follow his friend into the room. There were just a few standing lamps

and one small bulb on the ceiling to provide light. Ten life-size dummies, or mannequins, each one wearing a different war uniform, stood in the dim room. As Hakeem walked by a mannequin, the overhead light flickered. At that moment, Hakeem looked at the mannequin's face. The flickering light made the shadows over its eyes jump. Hakeem gasped.

6. "What is it?" asked Malcolm.

"Watch," said Hakeem. They stood in front of the mannequin and waited. After a minute, the light overhead flickered.

"Whoa!" said Malcolm. "That looked like he was shifting his eyes!"

"That explains what Sammy saw," said Hakeem. "What about the noises?"

7. Malcolm started leaning from side to side and walked around the room like a duck. Each time he shifted his weight to one side, a floorboard creaked. As he wobbled around the room, the floorboards creaked and moaned.

Hakeem laughed. "This place is great!" he said. "I'm so glad my brother didn't scare me away!

10. What did Hakeem's brother Gerard warn him about?

Ⓐ The old war uniforms room

Ⓑ The old records room

Ⓒ The old costume dummies room

Ⓓ The old museum room

This question has two parts. Answer Part A, then answer Part B.

11. Part A: Which statement in paragraph 2 shows that Hakeem's mother does not trust Sammy?

Ⓐ Gerard, stop scaring your brother

Ⓑ Hakeem, there is no such thing as ghosts

Ⓒ I'm sure there is a logical explanation to those noises

Ⓓ That's just Sammy's imagination getting out of hand

Part B: Who else in the story says the same thing regarding Sammy?

Ⓐ Gerard

Ⓑ Mr. Orwell

Ⓒ Malcolm

Ⓓ County historian

12. What word best matches the description of Hakeem in paragraph three?

Ⓐ Honest

Ⓑ Happy

Ⓒ Brave

Ⓓ Angry

13. What word best matches the description of Gerard in paragraph three?

Ⓐ Happy

Ⓑ Honest

Ⓒ Angry

Ⓓ Brave

14. What made the mannequin's eyes look like they were moving?

Ⓐ The few standing lamps

Ⓑ The creaky floorboards

Ⓒ The flickering overhead bulb

Ⓓ The old uniform

15. What definition best matches the meaning of the word "dim" in paragraph five?

Ⓐ Badly lit

Ⓑ Dusty

Ⓒ Empty

Ⓓ Crowded

16. Why did Hakeem laugh in paragraph seven?

Ⓐ Because Malcolm walked like a duck in the old uniform room

Ⓑ Because the old uniform room was haunted

Ⓒ Because his brother, Gerard, lied to him about the old uniform room

Ⓓ Because he found out the old uniform room was not haunted

17. Which of the following statements tells the main idea of this story?

Ⓐ It is important to be brave

Ⓑ Appearances can be deceiving

Ⓒ Trust people older than you

Ⓓ Historical museums are haunted

18. What is another name for the life-size dummies in the old war uniforms room?

Ⓐ life-like people

Ⓑ uniform holders

Ⓒ mannequins

Ⓓ haunted figures

Questions 19 -28 pertain to the following passage:

The State Fair of Texas

Manuela wrote the following journal entry about her visit to the annual State Fair in Dallas, Texas.

October 11, 2009

My father woke me up early, at 6 a.m., so we could get to the Texas State Fair in time to get a good parking spot. This was my first visit to the fair. I am eight-years-old, and I live near Dallas, where the fair is held every year from late September to early October. We quickly ate breakfast. Dad put his coffee in a thermos cup so he could finish it on the drive.

It only took us 20 minutes to get to the fairgrounds, but we had to wait for 30 minutes to get a parking space! By the time we got into the fair, it was almost 8 a.m. We were at the fair to see my cousin Gloria with her prize goats. Gloria is four years older than I am. She lives on a farm near Austin where her family raises goats and sheep. They use the animals' milk to make cheese and the sheep's wool to make yarn. Gloria has five goats, and she was showing two of them.

Gloria's goats are Nubian. They have short hair and very long, dangly ears. Gloria's two goats are named Maja and Henry.

Maja, a girl, is white with black and tan spots. Henry, a boy, is mostly black with white feet and a white spot on his throat. Gloria was judged on how her goats looked and how they behaved in the ring. Gloria had washed and brushed both goats so they had very shiny coats. The goats were not very tall. Maja's head came up to my chest, and Henry was tall enough to rest his chin on my shoulder. Gloria said they were supposed to look well fed, but not fat.

"No ribs showing and no belly sticking out," she said as she walked Maja around the pen.

The goats also were judged on how well they behaved in front of the judges. Gloria got points if the goats followed her and did everything she told them to do. She lost points if the goats did not follow her or ran away. Gloria said that last year, her friend's goat got only halfway around the ring before a whistle scared him and he ran back to the gate.

Finally, it was time for Gloria to show her goats. She brought out Maja first. Maja was wearing a harness with a leash attached to it. Maja followed Gloria very quietly until they reached the judge's table. Then Maja began to bleat. At first, she bleated softly, but then she got louder. By the time Gloria brought her back to the gate, Maja was bleating very loudly.

I wondered if the judges took away points if the goat was noisy while it was being shown. Henry was much better. He did everything Gloria told him to do without making a sound. I thought for sure Henry would get a prize.

After Gloria was finished, we waited for the judges to announce the prizes. We were so surprised when Maja got second place!

"I guess the judges understand goat," joked Gloria, as she showed off her prizes. Henry only got an honorable mention.

We had a great time at the fair. I learned a lesson from Maja. The squeaky wheel gets the grease after all!

19.

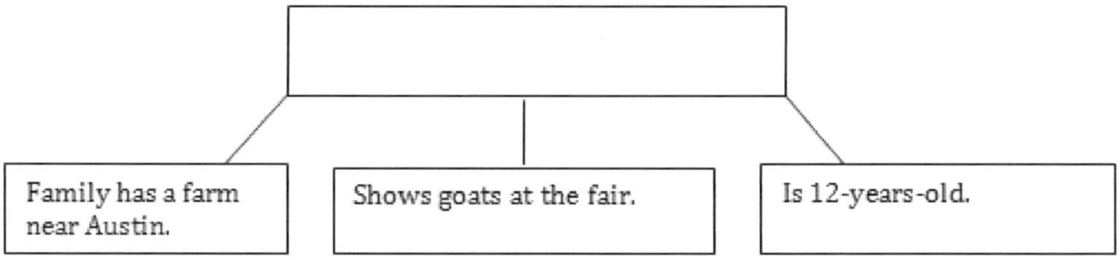

Which name goes into the box at the top of the diagram?

Ⓐ Maja

Ⓑ Gloria

Ⓒ Henry

Ⓓ Manuela

20. Where is the Texas State Fair held?

Ⓐ Dallas

Ⓑ Austin

Ⓒ Houston

Ⓓ San Antonio

21. What does Gloria's family make on their farm?

Ⓐ Sheep and goats

Ⓑ Wool and sheep

Ⓒ Goats and wool

Ⓓ Cheese and yarn

This question has two parts. Answer Part A, then answer Part B.

22. Part A: How many goats does Gloria have?

Ⓐ Two

Ⓑ Three

Ⓒ Four

Ⓓ Five

Part B: How many goats is Gloria showing?

Ⓐ Two

Ⓑ Three

Ⓒ Four

Ⓓ Five

23. How are the goats judged?

Ⓐ By their looks and behavior

Ⓑ By their looks and sounds

Ⓒ By their sounds and ears

Ⓓ By their weight and sounds

24. The chart shows the order of some events from the story.

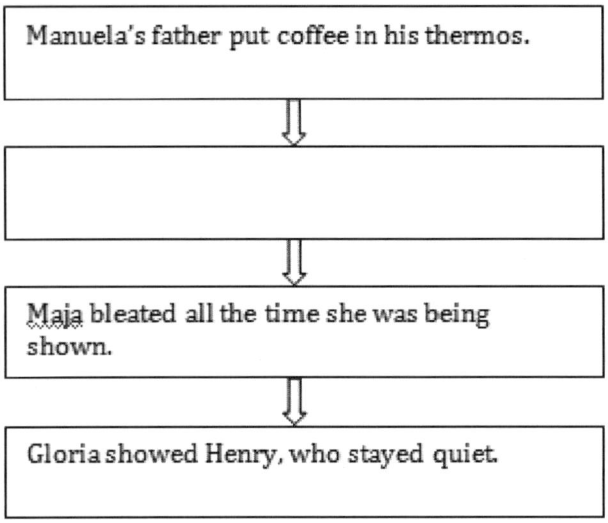

Which event belongs in the empty box?

Ⓐ Manuela had a great time at the fair

Ⓑ Manuela got up at 6 a.m.

Ⓒ Manuela and her father waited half-an-hour to park

Ⓓ Gloria won two prizes for her goats

25. Manuela woke up at 6 a.m. for the fair. How many hours later was it before she got into the fair?

Ⓐ Two

Ⓑ Three

Ⓒ Two and a half

Ⓓ One and a half

26. How did Gloria describe a goat that is well fed but not too fat?

Ⓐ "Nice and plump"

Ⓑ "Just right"

Ⓒ "No ribs showing and no belly sticking out"

Ⓓ "Good tone and a nice shape"

27. Why was Manuela sure that Henry would get a prize?

Ⓐ Because he was so fat

Ⓑ Because he was so quiet

Ⓒ Because his coat was so shiny

Ⓓ Because he was so tall

28. What does "the squeaky wheel gets the grease" mean in this story?

Ⓐ Manuela had a great day at the fair

Ⓑ Henry got an award for being quiet

Ⓒ Gloria won two prizes for her goats

Ⓓ Maja was noisy, but she still won a prize

Questions 29 - 34 pertain to the following invitation:

Patricio Suarez

Come To My Birthday Party

When: Saturday, February 12, 2011 at 2 p.m.

Where: 1234 Main Street, El Paso

Bring: Your bathing suit

Reply: (915) 123-4567

29. Who is having a party?

Ⓐ Saturday February

Ⓑ Main Street

Ⓒ Your bathing suit

Ⓓ Patricio Suarez

30. Where is the location for the party?

Ⓐ (915) 123-4567

Ⓑ 1234 Main Street, El Paso

Ⓒ Suarez@abcde.com

Ⓓ Your bathing suit

31. What time is the party?

Ⓐ 2 p.m.

Ⓑ 11 a.m.

Ⓒ 3 p.m.

Ⓓ 1 p.m.

32. What kind of party is it?

Ⓐ Welcome home

Ⓑ Anniversary

Ⓒ Graduation

Ⓓ Birthday

33. How should you respond to this invitation?

Ⓐ Just show up at the party

Ⓑ Either call or email

Ⓒ Don't got to the party

Ⓓ Just tell Patricio at school

34. What is the main activity at the party?

Ⓐ Playing games

Ⓑ Eating cake

Ⓒ Swimming

Ⓓ Horseback riding

Questions 35 - 40 pertain to the following passage:

When I Am Sick

At least once a year my nose gets red,
and I cough and sniffle and sneeze.
My mother tucks me into bed
with a heavy blanket, so I won't freeze.
She feeds me a teaspoon of medicine,
it is purple and very thick.
It tastes like grapes and drips on my chin,
but it makes me feel better quick.
My mother stays home from work,
she reads me books and lets me watch TV.
I do not like feeling sick,
but I love having my mother all to me.

35. What kind of illness is the author describing in the first two lines?

Ⓐ Stomach flu

Ⓑ Headache

Ⓒ Mumps

Ⓓ Cold

36. What does the mother do when the author is sick?

Ⓐ Takes her temperature

Ⓑ Tucks her into bed

Ⓒ Calls the doctor

Ⓓ Makes tea

37. What does the medicine look and taste like?

Ⓐ Purple, thin, grapes and apples

Ⓑ Purple, thick, grapes and apples

Ⓒ Purple, thick, and grapes

Ⓓ Purple, thin, and grapes

38. What does the author like about being sick?

Ⓐ She gets her mother's full attention

Ⓑ She gets to stay home from school

Ⓒ She gets to watch TV

Ⓓ Her mother reads her books

39. Which words in this poem rhyme?

Ⓐ The first word of every line

Ⓑ The last word of every line

Ⓒ The last word of every third line

Ⓓ The last word of every other line

40. How often does the author get sick?

Ⓐ Almost never

Ⓑ At least once a year

Ⓒ Twice a year

Ⓓ At least once every few years

Thank You

We at Mometrix would like to extend our heartfelt thanks to you, our friend and patron, for allowing us to play a part in your journey. It is a privilege to serve people from all walks of life who are unified in their commitment to building the best future they can for themselves.

The preparation you devote to these important testing milestones may be the most valuable educational opportunity you have for making a real difference in your life. We encourage you to put your heart into it—that feeling of succeeding, overcoming, and yes, conquering will be well worth the hours you've invested.

We want to hear your story, your struggles and your successes, and if you see any opportunities for us to improve our materials so we can help others even more effectively in the future, please share that with us as well. **The team at Mometrix would be absolutely thrilled to hear from you!** So please, send us an email (support@mometrix.com) and let's stay in touch.

Online Resources

Due to our efforts to try to keep this book to a manageable length, we've created a link that will give you access to all of your online resources:

mometrix.com/resources719/ssncg3elarwb

It's Your Moment, Let's Celebrate It!

Share your story @mometrixtestpreparation